NO BULL ~~NOBLE~~ REVIEW™

US GOV'T. & POLITICS

For use with the AP®
US Gov't. & Politics Exam

A no-nonsense approach to prepare for
class and the big tests

by Jeremy Klaff & Harry Klaff

About the Authors

Harry Klaff taught high school social studies in the New York City public schools system for 34 years. In 1993, he was the honored recipient of the John Bunzel Memorial Award as NYC's social studies teacher of the year. As a member of city-wide Justice Resource Center, he helped write numerous curricula in law-related education. For many years, he created the annual Model City Council project, in which students took over New York's City Hall for a day-long simulation exercise.

Jeremy Klaff has been teaching AP History classes for over a decade. His website, www.mrklaff.com has been utilized by teachers and students across the country for review materials as well as original social studies music. Jeremy has published Document Based Questions for Binghamton University's Women's History website, womhist.binghamton.edu. He has conducted staff developments for "Entertainment in Education" at both the high school and college level. In 2006, he was included in the Who's Who of American Teachers.

©2013 by No Bull Review™ Reproduction in whole or in part without written permission of the publisher is strictly prohibited.

This book might contain product names, trademarks, or registered trademarks. All trademarks in this book are property of their respective owners. If used, they are for non-biased use, and we do not encourage or discourage use of said product or service. Any term suspected of being a trademark will be properly capitalized.

The authors of this book make no warranties based on misinformation, or information excluded from these pages. The author shall not be liable for any positive or negative test scores achieved.

Special thanks to Petro Macrigiane and Eric Begun

Cover Artwork by Stephanie Strack

Table of Contents

Introduction to the No Bull Approach 4
The Basics, the Constitution, and Federalism 5
    Review Questions 15
    Free-Response Questions 17
    Answers and Explanations 18
Political Beliefs and Behaviors 19
    Review Questions 24
    Free-Response Questions 26
    Answers and Explanations 27
Political Parties, Interest Groups, and the Media 28
    Review Questions 37
    Free-Response Questions 39
    Answers and Explanations 40
The Legislative Branch 41
    Review Questions 50
    Free-Response Questions 52
    Answers and Explanations 53
The Executive Branch 54
    Review Questions 62
    Free-Response Questions 64
    Answers and Explanations 65
The Judicial Branch 66
    Review Questions 71
    Free-Response Questions 73
    Answers and Explanations 74
The Executive Branch Bureaucracy and Public Policy 75
    Review Questions 81
    Free-Response Questions 83
    Answers and Explanations 84
Civil Rights and Civil Liberty 85
    Review Questions 92
    Free-Response Questions 94
    Answers and Explanations 95
Practice Test One 96
Practice Test Two 110
No Bull Review Sheet 125

The No Bull Approach

No Bull Review…"because your review book shouldn't need a review book!"

> Go to page 125 and cut out my No Bull Review Sheets. Use them to help you study.

This review book is the most concise and to the point review available for US Government and Politics. Our goal here is to give you everything you need to know for class and exams. Sometimes review books can be full of material that you just don't need to know. Or, they give explanations that are just as long as the ones found in the textbooks. The No Bull approach is to cut through the fat, and give you what you want.

We, as authors of No Bull Review, are teachers. For years, we have been speaking to students to find out what you want in a review book. The answer? No Bull. You want the facts, clear and to the point. And…you want review questions. Lots of them.

At the end of this book you will find an intense review sheet. If you know all of the terms and definitions on the No Bull Review Sheet, you should find success.

The practice questions in this book are our own creation, and are based on the style of questions commonly used in the curriculum. They are questions that evaluate the most important themes of US Government and Politics.

We hope you enjoy the No Bull approach. Thank you, and best of luck.

– No Bull Review

The Basics, the Constitution, and Federalism

In addition to learning about the Constitution and federalism, this chapter will give you the basics of government that you need to know for understanding the rest of the course. After a weak Articles of Confederation, the United States adopted a strong Constitution, which went into effect in 1789. The Constitution established a system of separation of powers and checks and balances. Although it made the federal (national) government very strong, states retained some sovereignty because of federalism. Although the power of states' rights would be debated for a century, federal supremacy has become accepted.

HERE IS WHAT YOU NEED TO KNOW:
Definition: Direct Democracy and Republic

Direct democracy is a bare-bones democracy where all qualified people have a voice in government and can vote on issues. This was a form of democracy in Ancient Greece, where male citizens governed. But it wouldn't work here...too many voices. The US has a *representative democracy* where people are elected to serve the needs of the citizens. In this *republic*, voters have power, but those elected to office are the ones who govern.

Decisions in a democracy are influenced by majority rule, or where actions reflect the opinions of the majority. Although *majoritarianism* might lead some to fear a "tyranny of the majority," the Constitution looks to protect the rights of all.

Question: In what ways do those elected represent themselves?
Answer: **T-D-P-P**

1. **Trustee** - This is a representative (or other elected official) who makes their political decisions based upon the greater common good, and doesn't necessarily do what their constituents (people they represent who voted them in) want. Their job is to work for the national interest. When representatives vote their conscience and ideology, it's known as the *attitudinal view* of voting. Remember: "My constituents *trust* my judgment."

2. **Delegate** - Representatives acting as delegates make decisions that reflect the desires of their constituents. A delegate is supposed to refrain from voting their own conscience. They comply with the *representational view* of voting.

3. **Politico** - A politico is a combination of the above representative models, or someone who does what he or she wants to until the constituents come calling!

4. **Partisan** - A partisan votes along with their political party. Remember: P for Partisan, P for party. When representatives vote to make their colleagues happy, it's known as the *organizational view* of voting. This has become increasingly evident in recent years.

Question: What do I need to know about the Declaration of Independence of July 4, 1776?
Answer:

1. It stated that, "all men are created equal" with three *unalienable rights*..."life, liberty, and the pursuit of happiness." These are Enlightenment ideas stemming from ***John Locke*** in particular.

2. The document included a long list of grievances against King George III.

3. At the end, there was a formal declaration of war against Great Britain.

The document declared independence, and that the United States was a free nation. NOTE: The Declaration did not contain a blueprint for government as the Constitution would. It did, however, set a precedent for liberty and equality which would later be incorporated into the legal system.

Question: What were some of the weaknesses of the Articles of Confederation?

After winning the Revolutionary War, the new United States had to form a government. Instead of drawing up a strong Constitution, they lived by the weak Articles of Confederation from 1781-1789. The Articles gave more power to the state governments, than it did the *federal (or central/national) government*. Such a distribution of power is called *decentralized power*. Here are some weaknesses to know:

1. Each state could coin its own money
2. No Executive Branch existed
3. No regulation of interstate commerce (from one state to another)
4. No national court system
5. No army
6. 9 of the 13 states had to agree to pass a law
7. All of the states needed to agree to pass an amendment
8. Inefficient taxation system

Definition: Shays' Rebellion, 1786-87

Daniel Shays' Rebellion was a Massachusetts uprising where farmers protested imprisonment for debt, lack of currency, and high taxes. It showed just how weak the Articles were, as there was no national army to put down the insurrection. The Massachusetts state militia eventually ended the violence, but plans to scrap the Articles intensified.

Definition: Philadelphia Convention

Fifty-five delegates assembled in Philadelphia in 1787. ***Their intention was not to make a Constitution***, but rather to ***amend*** the Articles of Confederation. Of course as it turned out, they would indeed write a new Constitution here.

You need to know that the Constitution is the document Americans live by, and it is essentially the rules of the game of government. The Constitution has the final say and is the highest law of the land. As we shall see, it was a bundle of compromises.

Definition: Virginia Plan, New Jersey Plan, and Great Compromise of the Convention

Remember: In a republic, people are elected by the people, to serve the people. The Great Compromise created our modern day Legislative Branch that makes laws. It was based on:

The Virginia Plan - James Madison wanted a *bicameral (2 house)* legislature based upon population. The greater the population, the more representatives a state would have.

The New Jersey Plan - William Paterson wanted representation to be equal so the small states would not be under-represented.

The Great Compromise (Connecticut Compromise of Roger Sherman - Created the current bicameral (2 house) legislature where the *House of Representatives* is based upon population, and the *Senate* has equal representation (2 Senators per state). A *census* (described in depth later) taken every ten years determines state population and representation.

Definition: 3/5th Compromise

But wait a minute! If the House is based on

population, how should the United States count slaves?

The Northern states wanted slaves to count for taxation, but not representation.

The Southern states wanted slaves to count for representation but not taxation.

The 3/5 Compromise stated that each slave would count as 3/5th of a person for both taxation and representation.

Note: The Trans-Atlantic Slave Trade could continue until 20 years after the Constitution (1808).

Definition: Commercial Compromise and Commerce Clause

The Northern states wanted to regulate interstate commerce, and tax imports and exports.

The Southern states feared export taxes, as they exported a lot of farm goods.

The compromise gave the federal government the power to regulate interstate commerce, and tax imports but not exports. This tax on imports is referred to as a *tariff*. Sometimes the term customs-duties is used instead.

Such regulation of trade can be found in the Constitution's *Commerce Clause*, where Congress is given the power to regulate commerce between the states, with foreign nations, and with Native American tribes. Controlling interstate commerce is a major component of federalism (explained this chapter).

Definition: Federalists/Anti-Federalists

Federalists favored the Constitution and were led by James Madison, George Washington, and Alexander Hamilton.

Anti-Federalists were scared that the Constitution might put too much power into the hands of the government. They were led by James Winthrop, John Hancock, George Clinton, and George Mason.

Note: Thomas Jefferson (in France), and John Adams (in Great Britain) were not present for the debate.

Question: What was written to persuade New Yorkers and other doubters to ratify the Constitution?

Answer: ***The Federalist*** (or ***The Federalist Papers***) was a series of 85 published essays that argued the need for a strong Constitution.

Alexander Hamilton wrote most of them. John Jay wrote a few on foreign policy. But, James Madison wrote the most famous one, *Federalist #10* (see next).

Definition: *Federalist #10*

James Madison contended that the Constitution would work in a very large republic. He said that a strong union would be able to control tyrannical *factions*, or groups, who were out for their own good. He believed that a republic that serves the public good would eliminate the effects of dangerous factions.

Also famous is Madison's *#51*, where he advocates for checks and balances and separation of powers to protect against abuse of power.

Definition: Bill of Rights, 1791

Ultimately the Constitution was ratified (approved) in 1788 when 9 of the 13 states agreed. But the promise for a Bill of Rights was critical. It would become the first 10 Amendments (changes/additions) to the Constitution. The Bill of Rights protected important freedoms such as speech, right to bear arms, due process, prevention of cruel and unusual punishment, and the right to an attorney.

The ones you need to know the most are in the No Bull Review Sheet, and will be addressed in the chapter on civil liberties.

NOTE: Nowhere in the Bill of Rights does it speak about economic equality. Although "equality of opportunity" is encouraged, "equality of result" is not.

Question: What purpose does each of the three branches have?

Answer: The idea of ***separation of powers*** came from Enlightenment philosopher, Baron de Montesquieu. He believed that the powers of government should be balanced between the:

1. **Legislative Branch** - Makes the laws. The United States has a bicameral (two house) Congress composed of the ***House of Representatives*** (435 members) which is based on population, and the ***Senate*** which has 2 members for each state (100 members). The Speaker of the House is the leader of the House of Representatives. The Vice President can preside over the Senate, though rarely does. A President pro tempore is chosen by the Senate instead.

2. **Executive Branch** - Enforces, or executes the laws to ensure people obey them. The President leads this branch. In a state, this would be the Governor. For a city, it would be the Mayor. If the President can't perform his or her duties, the Vice President becomes "Acting President." If the President dies in office, the Vice President becomes the President. The President has an extensive bureaucracy which supports this branch.

3. **Judicial Branch** - Interprets the laws to make sure they are fair and just. ***It protects the Constitution as the highest law of the land.*** No laws can overrule the Constitution. The highest court is the Supreme Court of the US.

Question: What are specific major powers of each branch?

Answer: We will go more in depth later, but here are the basics for now:

1. **Legislative Branch's Two Houses** - Makes laws, approves Presidential appointments, overrides vetoes, approves treaties, declares war, regulates interstate trade, and impeaches certain federal officials including the President.

2. **Executive Branch's President** - Commander-in-Chief of the military, signs and vetoes laws, pardons people to forgive their federal crimes, makes treaties, appoints government officials, recommends laws to Congress, and delivers the State of the Union Address.

3. **Judicial Branch's Supreme Court** - Decides if legislation is in line with the US Constitution. They can settle the disputes of state vs. state. The Supreme Court can strike down federal (national government) laws, as well as high state court decisions.

Question: What are the qualifications to hold major office?

Answer:

1. **House of Representatives** - Must be 25 years old, a US citizen for 7 years, and a resident of the state where serving. The term is 2 years.

2. **Senate** - Must be 30 years old, a US citizen for 9 years, and a resident of the state where serving. The term is 6 years.

3. **President/Vice President** - Must be 35 years old, a ***natural-born citizen***, and a US resident for 14 years. Each term in office is 4 years. Today, Representatives and Senators are elected by the people, and the President is chosen by ***electors*** (explained later).

4. **Supreme Court Justices** - No requirements. Appointed for life by the President, and confirmed by the Senate. ***This life appointment is supposed to free justices from political pres-***

sures, like those experienced by elected officials.

Definition: Federalism

Federalism is the division of power between the state and federal governments. According to Article I, Section 8 of the Constitution, the Congress has *delegated, or enumerated, powers* including declaring war and coining money. According to the **Tenth Amendment**, states have *reserved powers*. This means they are reserved the right to control other things, such as education, marriage, and driving laws. Some powers are shared, such as taxation. These are called *concurrent powers*. Here is what you need to know about the basics of federalism:

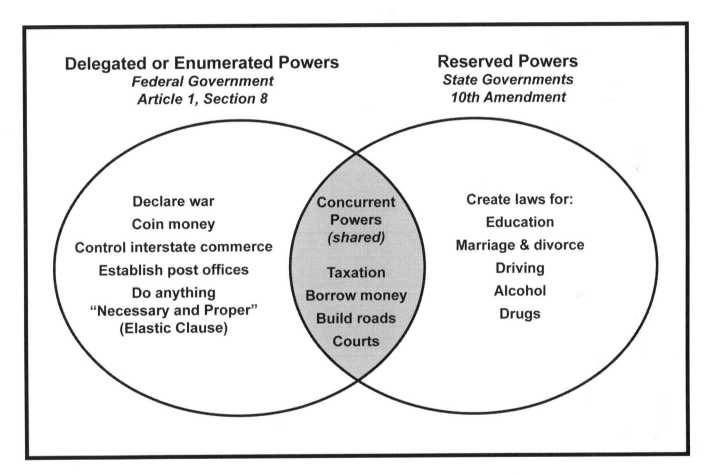

★Note: An incredibly common error is for students to mix up <u>division of powers</u> and <u>separation of powers</u>. *Don't do that! Division of powers* refers to Federalism, and the "division of powers" between the federal and state governments. The word federal is right in the term! *Separation of powers* deals with the three branches of the national/federal government.

Definition: Elastic Clause

Congress also has a delegated power to do anything **"necessary and proper."** This allows the Constitution to grow over time, so it doesn't become a dated document. This power is found in the Elastic Clause (Article I, Section 8, Clause 18). Use of the *Elastic Clause* is indicative of a *loose construction/interpretation* of the Constitution, and gives government more power to legislate. So let's say the government wants to pass a bill on internet reform. There was no internet in 1789, but today, making such a law would be considered "necessary and proper." ***Strict construction/interpretation*** would be the opposite, and would limit the government's power.

Note: Loose interpretation, or ***implied powers***, can be used by all three branches of government. The Elastic Clause itself is a Congressional entity.

Question: In the first 100 years of the United States, were there arguments over states' rights?

Yes. Until the Civil War, the states questioned the extent of the federal government's power. Thomas Jefferson and James Madison wrote the Kentucky and Virginia Resolutions challenging the federal government's Alien and Sedition Acts of 1798 (which limited civil liberties such as freedom of speech). Also, John C. Calhoun asserted that states could declare controversial laws, such as tariffs c1828, ***null and void***. However, since the Civil War, the national government has asserted its supremacy.

MORE ON FEDERALISM AND THE STATES
Definition: Dual Federalism and Cooperative Federalism

Hungry? Let's have some cake. ***Dual federalism*** is like a layer cake where you have distinct separation between the icing and the cake. In this type of federalism there is EXACT agreement as to what the states control and what the national government does.

Cooperative federalism is like a marble cake, where the chocolate and vanilla are blurred together. More apparent since the 1930s, in this type of federalism, the national, state, and local governments share the responsibility of solving problems. For example, during Franklin D. Roosevelt's New Deal (plan to get the US out of the Great Depression), the states were required to cooperate with the federal government in distributing money for localized projects.

Question: What types of federal grants should I know?

In ***fiscal federalism***, money from the central government is allocated to lower levels in the form of grants. ***Grants-in-aid*** occur when money from the federal government is distributed to the states for projects. You need to know:

1. ***Block grants*** - These are general lump sums of money given to states for general purposes, such as spending on schools and libraries. Local politicians have a great deal of leeway as to how this money is spent, and it is their preferred form of grants.

From 1972-1986, ***revenue-sharing*** took place, where tax dollars went to the states for general purposes, or for almost anything they wanted. Today's block grants are smaller in size.

2. ***Categorical grants*** - This is money that has to be spent on specific categories, or projects. There's often a ***formula*** associated with these grants, as a state's wealth and demographics (population composition) can factor into the size of the grant. Also, the states usually have to match part of the grant with their own money. For example, in the Federal-Aid Highway Act of 1956, about 90% of the national highway system was funded by the federal government. The rest was matched by the states. States and cities could also receive categorical grants to help fight crime, flooding, and pollution.

Definition: Entitlements

One type of grant is an ***entitlement grant***, which gives money directly to individuals. Social Security and Medicare are entitlements received by older Americans (both explained later). Other important entitlements include welfare financial support and Medicaid health care for low-income Americans.

NOTE: ***The Welfare Reform Act of 1996*** (The Personal Responsibility and Work Opportunity Reconciliation Act) allows states and counties to run their own welfare programs and determine how they want to bring people into the workforce. Thus, the states can use the grant as they see fit. The act limited the duration of welfare benefits, and encouraged states to help people find jobs.

Definition: Social Security

Probably the most well-known entitlement program is Social Security. Created as part of Franklin D. Roosevelt's New Deal in 1935, this was a plan to help older Americans cope with the Great Depression.

Though there are other benefits associated with Social Security, most of the money still goes to older Americans. Today, the way it works is, the paychecks of younger people are taxed, and that money is then allocated to older people (who had put money into the fund when they were younger). However, today there's a large problem with the ***graying of America***, as "Baby Boomers" (those born right after World War II) are living longer. Because of this, too much money is being taken out of Social Security, and in the future, there may be not enough cash coming in to sustain the program.

Definition: Mandate

"Clean your room, or you won't get your allowance!" Your parent just gave you a mandate. A ***mandate*** is an order from a higher authority to do something, or you won't get your money. In the case of federalism, it means that the federal government is giving aid, but with strings attached.

Sometimes the government gives orders without giving money. This is called an ***unfunded mandate***. These mandates try to serve the national interest. For example the Clean Air Act of 1970 ordered that cities comply with new healthy standards. It was up to the states to pay the bill. The same can be said about the Americans with Disabilities Act (ADA), which ordered all state public facilities to comply with federal standards for the disabled.

Definition: New Federalism and Devolution

Because the US government ballooned in size after the Progressive Era (c1900-1920) and the New Deal (c1933-1939), there has been an outcry to return power to the states. This ***devolution*** of power, as it's called, is known as New Federalism. Ronald Reagan supported devolution. As the federal, state, and local governments compete for power and taxpayer dollars, it can be referred to as ***competitive federalism.***

Question: What landmark Supreme Court cases debated state vs. federal power?

Answer: Each of the following cases led to a strengthening of the federal (national) government. You need to know that according to the Constitution's ***supremacy clause***, all federal laws and decisions are superior to those made by the states.

1. ***McCulloch v. Maryland***, 1819 - Because the State of Maryland wanted to get rid of a branch of the Bank of the United States, it put a tax on banknotes. Chief Justice John Marshall

ruled that a state could not tax a federal entity. He said that the power to tax meant "the power to destroy."

2. *Gibbons* v. *Ogden*, **1824** - Thomas Gibbons claimed that an act of Congress permitted him steamship commerce between New York and New Jersey. Aaron Ogden was issued an exclusive ferrying license from New York State. Marshall said that Gibbons had the legitimate license, because the federal government regulated interstate commerce (commerce between different states). Thus, Marshall upheld the supremacy of the federal government.

NOTE: To this day, the issue of interstate commerce pops up in federal courts.

Definition: Denied Powers

To protect against tyranny, the Founding Fathers denied some powers to both the federal and state governments.

The federal government can't grant titles of nobility, or levy export taxes. They also can't pass **ex-post facto laws**. This means that if you did something legal on Tuesday, and a law was passed on Thursday against what you were doing, you wouldn't be breaking the law for your Tuesday actions. Finally, there are no **Bills of Attainder**, which if allowed, could imprison someone without a trial.

States are denied the right to enter into treaties with foreign nations. They also can't print money or tax imports or exports.

Question: How can the Constitution be changed?

Answer: Although very difficult, the Constitution can be altered through **amendments** (changes or additions). An amendment becomes a part of the Constitution, and therefore becomes part of the highest law of the land. There are several methods for proposing and ratifying an amendment, but only one is generally used.

Proposal Process:

1. 2/3 vote of each House (used for all amendments). OR…

2. Congress calls for a national constitutional convention at the request of 2/3 of the states (never used).

Ratification Process:

1. 3/4 of the state legislatures have to ratify it (used for all but one). OR…

2. Ratified by 3/4 of state conventions. Only the Twenty-First Amendment used this method. It was ratified when 3/4 of state conventions voted to bring back the sale of alcohol.

Thus, the amendment process has been a great example of federalism at work, as both the states and the federal government are in cooperation.

Question: What amendments do I need to know?

There are 27 amendments. As stated above, the Bill of Rights provided the first ten at the same time in 1791. The amendments most relevant to the curriculum are in the No Bull Review Sheet.

Definition: Checks and Balances

Each branch looks over the shoulders of the other two to make sure that there are no abuses of power. You need to know certain checks and balances, of which we will later go into greater detail. But for now:

If the President doesn't like a bill, he or she can *veto* to prevent it from becoming a law. The Legislative Branch can then override that veto with a 2/3 vote from each house. The

President appoints federal jobs such as Supreme Court justices, and the Senate approves these appointments. The President can make treaties, but the Senate must approve them. The Judicial Branch can strike down actions of both the President and Congress. Here is an illustration of the most important checks to know:

	LEGISLATIVE	EXECUTIVE	JUDICIAL
LEGISLATIVE CHECKS		1. Can override vetoes by 2/3 vote 2. Senate can refuse to confirm a Presidential appointment	1. Can change the size of the Supreme Court
EXECUTIVE CHECKS	1. Can veto bills 2. Can call Congress into special session		1. Appoints Supreme Court justices 2. Grants pardons and reprieves
JUDICIAL CHECKS	1. Can declare an act of Congress to be unconstitutional (judicial review)	1. Can declare an act of the President to be unconstitutional	

Definition: Unwritten Constitution

This term is used to describe things that happen in United States government procedure that's not written directly in the Constitution. Examples include political parties, judicial review, and nominating conventions. These are all big parts of American government. It's almost as if they are in the Constitution…but they're not!

Similarly, it's important to understand the difference between the ***formal and informal Constitution***. The only formal way to change the Constitution is by amending it. But, informally, the Constitution can be manipulated by using judicial review, the Elastic Clause, and creating political norms such as primaries and nominating conventions.

Definition: Pluralism

This is a theory on government where no one dominates the tools that shape policy. Both society and government are way too complex to be controlled by an elite. It's hard to put a finger on who is influencing policy, because so many different individuals and ideas shape the nation. Instead, there's continual competition, where many voices can be powerful enough to affect policy.

The Pluralist Theory differs from the ***Elitist Theory***. In Elitism, the decisions are made at the top with less regard for the common citizens. Master politicians and property owners are the ones in charge, as decisions are made with less regard for public opinion.

Review Questions

1. Which of the following describes a representative who feels he or she is responsible for conveying the thoughts of their constituents?
   A) Delegate
   B) Partisan
   C) Trustee
   D) Politico
   E) Liberal

2. Which statement is an example of how pluralism has affected United States government?
   A) The Supreme Court can overturn a decision
   B) Many different voices can alter public policy
   C) The Constitution successfully safeguards against the voice of factions
   D) Delegates don't always reflect the beliefs of their constituents
   E) The President can veto a bill

3. Which of the following was a weakness of the Articles of Confederation that was corrected by the Constitution?
   A) Ability to make amendments
   B) Federal control of interstate commerce
   C) Power to make treaties with foreign countries
   D) Ability to add more states to the union
   E) Presence of a national legislature

4. Which statement is true about cooperative federalism?
   A) It has the greatest amount of devolution of all types of federalism
   B) There are clear distinctions between the powers of the state and the national government
   C) Local governments have little-to-no power in decision-making
   D) Problems are solved at the national level and decisions trickle down to the states
   E) All levels of government share the responsibility of carrying out decisions and policy

5. Which of the following types of governments has the greatest degree of participation for the average citizen?
   A) Republic
   B) Monarchy
   C) Direct Democracy
   D) Confederation
   E) Dual Federalism

6. Which of the following is an enumerated power of the federal government?
   A) Laws regarding driving
   B) The legal alcohol limit for operating a boat
   C) Marriage and divorce laws
   D) Establishing a method to deliver mail
   E) Diploma requirements for high school graduation

7. Why do local politicians prefer block grants to categorical-formula grants?
   A) Block grants always offer much more money
   B) There is more leeway for politicians to spend block grants on what they want
   C) Categorical-formula grants are taxed at a much higher rate
   D) Block grants are matched by local governments
   E) Categorical-formula grants can be considered unconstitutional

8. Which of the following would be an example of loose interpretation of the Constitution?
   A) Utilization of the Elastic Clause
   B) Congress overriding of a Presidential veto
   C) State ratification of an amendment
   D) Impeachment of the President
   E) Refusing to pass an ex-post facto law

9. Which of the following is NOT a legal check and balance?
   A) The President can veto bills
   B) The Legislative Branch can increase the size of the Supreme Court
   C) The Senate confirms Presidential appointments
   D) The Judicial Branch can declare acts of Congress unconstitutional
   E) The House of Representatives can refuse to ratify a treaty

10. Where in today's government do we see the greatest impact of the Great Compromise of the Philadelphia Convention?
    A) The ability of the President to grant pardons and reprieves
    B) The granting of liberty to all men and women
    C) A bicameral legislature
    D) Separation of powers
    E) Reserved powers for the states

Free-Response Questions

I. After the Revolutionary War, a weak Articles of Confederation gave much power to individual states. However, the Articles created problems, and were replaced by a Constitution. Though debated, The Federalist Papers predicted that a strong central government would be successful in the newly formed United States.
   A. Explain two weaknesses of the Articles of Confederation, and how the Constitution looked to solve these weaknesses. [p. 6]
   B. Describe one main idea of James Madison's Federalist #10. [p. 7]
   C. Explain how both of the following could protect against tyranny:
     1. Checks and Balances [pp. 12-13]
     2. Federalism [pp. 9-10]

II. After winning the American Revolution, the newly formed United States looked to establish a new form of government that differed from the monarchy of Great Britain.
   A. Define direct democracy. [p. 5]
   B. Identify how a republic differs from direct democracy. [p. 5]
   C. Explain how two of the following conduct themselves in representation: [p. 5]
     • Trustee
     • Delegate
     • Partisan

Answers and Explanations

1. **A**. Elected officials who represent their constituents directly, and are accountable for working on policies which the people support, are acting as a *delegate*.

2. **B**. Pluralism is a theory of government where it's hard to put a finger on who influences policy because so many different individuals and ideas shape the nation.

3. **B**. The Articles of Confederation provided for a loose union of states. However, the Articles could do everything listed EXCEPT control interstate commerce. Other weaknesses included a lack of an army, and the ability to tax efficiently.

4. **E**. Cooperative federalism is like a marble cake, where the chocolate and vanilla are blurred together. More apparent since the 1930s, in this type of federalism, the federal, state, and local governments share the responsibility of solving problems. Clear distinctions would mean dual federalism, or a layer cake.

5. **C**. In a direct democracy, all citizens would have a say in government decision-making.

6. **D**. Enumerated, or delegated, powers are those bestowed on Congress. The creation of the postal service is one of these. Others include the regulation of interstate commerce, declaration of war, and coinage of money. The other choices were powers reserved for the states. Taxation is a shared, or concurrent, power of both the states and the federal government.

7. **B**. Block grants are lump sums of money given to states for general purposes, such as health services. Local politicians have a lot of leeway on how this money is spent.

8. **A**. The Elastic Clause allows Congress to do anything that is "necessary and proper." This permits Congress to pass a variety of laws that are not specifically listed in its delegated powers. This type of loose interpretation of the Constitution makes Congress stronger.

9. **E**. The House of Representatives doesn't ratify treaties. The Senate provides that check.

10. **C**. The Great Compromise created a bicameral (two house) legislature where the number of state representatives in the House of Representatives would be based on population, and the Senate would have equal representation for all states.

Political Beliefs and Behaviors

Everybody has an ideology, or set of beliefs. Your ideology is shaped by many factors, including your parents, friends, religion, ethnicity, and where you live. When you cast a ballot, your ideology will lead you to vote for certain candidates. But with so many issues out there, where will you stand? How do you know if a candidate will support your ideology? By studying the polls which measure public opinion, candidates learn just how to cater to the general public. However, despite having an ideology, far too many avoid taking part in the electoral process.

HERE IS WHAT YOU NEED TO KNOW:
Definition: Political ideology

You have one. Your friends have one. Your teachers have one as well. An ideology is your set of beliefs regarding what issues the government should support, and how it should rule.

Question: What types of ideologies do I need to know?

NOTE: Ideologies differ from person to person. The following are *generalizations*, as to the pure traditional beliefs of each.

1. **Liberal** - Favors liberty, equality, and wants as much progressive change as legally possible. Most Democrats frequent a more liberal ideology (but not always). They tend to support a woman's right to choose to have an abortion, same-sex marriage, freedom of speech and press, the rights of accused criminals, more government regulation of the economy, and universal health care.

2. **Conservative** - A conservative wants less change and reform than a liberal, and is satisfied with a limited role of the government. They tend to oppose government regulations on business, and support a free market. Socially, they agree with traditional moral and family values. They tend to be pro-life, favor the death penalty, and believe marriage is defined as between a man and a woman.

3. **Moderate** - Moderates are more liberal than a conservative, yet more conservative than a liberal. Being a "middle of the roader" is quite common, and these are the voters who often decide close elections. Many moderates consider themselves *independent*, or not part of a major political party.

3. **Libertarians** - These are people who tend to be conservative economically, but liberal on social issues. They want less government intervention in the lives of American citizens. The opposite view would be the Populist view. This ideology is economically liberal, yet Populists are social conservatives.

(See chart on next page)

Question: What shapes one's political attitude?

Answer: For decades, *political scientists such as V.O. Key, Jr.*, have been studying political behavior and public opinion's impact on elections. Through age and experience, people's political attitudes can change. The study of how ideology develops and is passed from one generation to another is called ***political socialization***. Below are factors that can shape political attitudes and one's public opinion. *Disclaimer: It should be noted that these are generalizations, and there are obviously many people of all backgrounds who vote for both the Democratic and Republican Parties.*

1. **Family impact** - Overwhelmingly, young adults tend to support the views of their par-

Generalizations of Liberals vs. Conservatives on Various Issues

ISSUE	LIBERAL VIEW	CONSERVATIVE VIEW
ABORTION	A woman should have the right to choose to have an abortion, and has a right to privacy.	Abortion is the murder of a human being, as life begins at conception. Taxpayer money should never be used to support abortion.
SAME-SEX MARRIAGE	Two people should be able to marry each other, regardless of which sex they are marrying.	Marriage is between a man and a woman.
ECONOMIC REGULATION	The economy must be overseen by the government to protect consumers from big business greed and manipulations in the market.	A laissez-faire, or government "hands off" approach, is necessary to ensure that markets are free and people and businesses have opportunities to accumulate capital and create jobs.
GUN CONTROL	The 2nd Amendment does not give people the right to own any type of weapon. There must be more aggressive background checks, and limiting of certain weapons and ammunition.	Gun control laws do not prevent criminals from obtaining weapons. People have the right to defend themselves.
DEATH PENALTY	The death penalty is murder and "cruel and unusual" punishment in violation of the 8th Amendment.	Executing someone who has committed murder is justified, and is neither cruel nor unusual.
TAXATION	Higher taxes are needed to pay for programs that help people. Liberals support higher taxes on the wealthy. Related: Liberals support welfare and Social Security.	Lower taxes, especially on the wealthy, create more money to be circulated through the economy. Furthermore, lower taxes on businesses encourage the creation of jobs. Conservatives want to reform Social Security and limit welfare entitlements.
HEALTH CARE	Quality health care should be available to every American.	Health care insurance should continue to operate freely. Enforcing cheaper government-run health care will lead to bad medicine and higher costs.

ents. Whether intentional or not, parents generally pass on their values to their children. Of political socialization factors, such as school, media, life experience, and peers, parents have the greatest influence.

2. **Race and Ethnicity** - Historically, immigrants, African Americans, and Hispanic Americans tend to be Democrats. This minority vote block has swayed Presidential elections.

3. **Religion** - Religion can work both ways. Religions which were discriminated against historically became liberal. Jews as well as Catholics historically voted Democratic. However, in recent decades they have been less loyal to the party. On the other side of the spectrum, today's Religious Right and Christian fundamentalists strongly oppose some liberal social values.

4. **Gender** - Like other historically discriminated groups, women overwhelmingly vote Democratic. Many women tend to be liberal on issues such as gun control, abortion, and helping the poor.

5. **Labor Unions** - Labor Unions who fight for the rights of workers lean towards the Democratic Party. Unions have historically contributed to Democratic candidates as well.

6. **Part of the country you reside** - As will be mentioned, throughout American History various regions of the country have voted predictably.

7. **Education and Occupation** - *People with more education are more likely to vote.* With so many graduates getting *liberal* arts degrees, greater education levels often make people liberal. However, those with advanced education generally get higher paying jobs…and wealthier Americans tend to be more conservative on economic matters.

Such a voter would be hard to predict, and would be considered a *cross-pressured voter*. With such a voter, personal background can influence how they feel on many issues. A cross-pressured voter can have liberal views on some issues, yet conservative views on other ones.

NOTE: In terms of voting in general, age becomes a factor. Especially in non-Presidential elections, older people are more likely to vote than younger people. This doesn't always mean they are more active in politics, it just means they make it their business to get to the polls to cast a ballot.

Question: Who votes?

Answer: **IMPORTANT** - Compared to other nations, many registered voters DON'T VOTE in the United States! Except in the high-profile, high-cost Presidential Elections (where a similar amount of men and women come out and vote).

NOTE: Some countries have very few elections, with even fewer candidates. That tends to pad their stats.

Question: What should I know about the history of voting?

1. In the Constitution, as it was written, people only voted for the House of Representatives. Senators were chosen by state legislatures until the **Seventeenth Amendment** permitted the people to vote for them in 1913. The President, still today, is chosen by the Electoral College, not directly by the people.

2. In the late eighteenth and early nineteenth centuries, very often you had to own property in order to vote. The states gradually phased this out by the mid-nineteenth century.

3. Voting was not secret until the Progressive Era (c1900), when the **Australian ballot** (secret ballot) became prevalent.

Question: What type of obstacles keep people from voting?

Answer:

1. Registration. Especially people who have just turned 18, finding time to register in the proper place can be an obstacle.

2. If people are out of town, they forget to cast *absentee ballots*.

3. States have different ways of proving you are who you are. In some states, bringing identification has become an issue that people don't want to deal with.

4. Although polls open early, and close late, people are busy with their lives and still don't vote.

5. In traditional blue and red states (in the media, Democrats are labeled "blue" and Repub-

licans "red"), many assume their vote doesn't matter, as the election isn't often in doubt.

6. Not everyone is permitted to vote in closed-primaries. Discussed later, one needs to be registered as a party member in this type of election.

7. One must be a legal citizen of the United States to vote (see page 91).

8. Obviously, people under the age of 18 can't vote. The age used to be 21, but the **Twenty-Sixth Amendment** changed that.

9. Felons who are in prison are denied voting privileges.

10. Lack of Trust. Many people are disillusioned with the government, and simply don't trust it. This type of apathy is common during controversial times such as war, economic decline, and social unrest.

11. Ballots are not in every language. By law, multilingual ballots must be provided by counties when the census shows that 5% of the population, or 10,000 voting-age citizens, are of a single-language minority group. So, depending on where someone lives, a ballot may not be in their native tongue.

Definition: Office-group ballot and party-column ballot

Office-group ballots list the candidates of all political parties by the office which is being contested.

Party-column ballots separate all of the offices into columns based on the political party. Therefore, one could merely choose one column and vote a *straight-ticket* of one party. This type of ballot discourages *ticket-splitting*, or voting for candidates from different parties on Election Day. *Independent voters*, or those who aren't affiliated with one party in particular, tend to be ticket-splitters.

Another ballot to be aware of is the *absentee ballot*, which can be filled out before the election if one can't make it to the *polling place* (location where people vote).

Question: What should I know about public opinion polls?

George Gallup was one of the pioneers of polling. His company, Gallup, is among the larger ones that still survey the public today. Polls measure what public opinion is on a variety of issues. Polls can influence members of Congress, especially those seeking reelection, to legislate along with the public will. You should know:

1. The people selected for a poll are usually in a **random sample**, meaning anyone in the public has a chance to be polled, or questioned. These days, much polling is done on the telephone.

2. The smaller the sample, the larger the **sampling error**, or the inaccuracy of the poll. Conversely, the larger the population polled, the more accurate the poll is. Usually, you'll see next to a poll the margin of error as a + or − 3%.

3. The poll should be unbiased and worded in a way that everyone can understand the question's objective.

4. *Exit polls* sample how people voted on Election Day, before the results come out. This can be dangerous, as in the Election of 2000, the media was too quick to call Florida in favor of Al Gore. Their data was based on inaccurate exit polling, as George W. Bush carried the state.

Definition: Activism

In addition to the fact that many people don't vote, many simply don't get involved. Still others, ***typically those with more education and of a higher economic status***, become politically active. Many movements begin as **_grassroots_**, or localized movements. Some ways people are active include:

1. Volunteer work for political or non-political organizations
2. Campaigning for a candidate
3. Giving time at a local religious center
4. Environmental activism
5. Taking action within the community to help with local problems

Review Questions

1. A poll with the smallest amount of sampling error would be one that
   A) samples half of a state's population
   B) only samples women
   C) targets minorities
   D) polls people who live in middle-class neighborhoods
   E) samples people who have signed up to be polled

2. Which of the following would BOTH be traditional liberal stances?
   A) Pro-life and pro-Social Security
   B) Pro-choice and anti-death penalty
   C) Pro-same sex marriage and pro-tax cuts on the wealthy
   D) Anti-universal health care and pro-gun control
   E) Pro-choice and anti-same sex marriage

3. Who is most likely to be a ticket-splitter?
   A) Democrat
   B) Republican
   C) Libertarian
   D) Socialist
   E) Independent

4. Compared to other countries, the United States
   A) turns out the greatest percentage of voters
   B) has a modest-to-low turnout rate for elections
   C) makes it compulsory to vote on Election Day
   D) has the fewest amount of offices up for grabs on Election Day
   E) has the fewest amount of political party choices

5. In the Constitution as it was written in 1787, which of the following would be the only office one could vote for *directly*?
   A) President
   B) Senator
   C) Vice President
   D) House of Representatives
   E) Secretary of State

6. *Traditionally*, the Republican Party would get more votes than Democrats from
   A) women
   B) African Americans
   C) Jewish Americans
   D) members of the Religious Right
   E) low-income Americans

7. Which of the following has the greatest impact on how a young person will vote?
   A) The ideology of the voter's parents
   B) Religion of the voter
   C) Job that the voter works
   D) Income level of the voter
   E) Number of years completed in college

8. Which change in voting came c1900?
   A) Removal of property ownership requirements
   B) Ability to vote for state legislators
   C) Creation of a secret ballot
   D) Invention of exit polls
   E) Voting for Vice Presidents on the same ticket as Presidents

9. Which of the following is true about people who have more education?
   A) They overwhelmingly vote Republican
   B) Almost all college graduates are liberals
   C) The greater the education, the more likely someone is to be an activist
   D) There is a greater chance for a college graduate to be part of a random sample
   E) Exit polls generally only interview those with a greater level of education

10. Someone with a purely conservative ideology would likely favor which economic strategy?
   A) Raising taxes
   B) Spending more money on social programs
   C) Spending to increase the size of the government
   D) Universal health care
   E) Laissez-faire and free trade

Free-Response Questions

I. An individual's ideology is influenced by many factors which can cause them to vote a certain way.
   A. Define political socialization. [p. 20]
   B. Explain how two of these factors can affect one's ideology: [pp. 20-21]
- Religion
- Education
- Ethnicity

   C. Identify one example of a cross-pressured voter. [p. 21]

II. Liberals and conservatives have battled each other since the founding of the United States. Whether it was the 1790s, or the 1990s, these two ideologies have clashed on issues ranging from the founding of a national bank, to abortion. They have also evolved into America's major modern-day political parties.
   A. Identify what is meant by the terms liberal and a conservative. [p. 19]
   B. Describe the differences between traditional liberal and conservative opinions concerning three of the following issues. [p. 20]
- Abortion
- Economic regulation
- Gun control
- Death Penalty

   C. Identify one polling technique that is used to measure public opinion. [p. 22]

Answers and Explanations

1. **A**. The larger the sample, the smaller the sampling error. Usually only a thousand to two thousand people are polled. Polling half of the state would be abnormal, but would truly knock down sampling error.

2. **B**. Pro-choice on abortion and anti-death penalty are traditional liberal views.

3. **E**. Independent voters are hard to predict, and often decide elections. Ticket-splitters are those who vote for different parties on a ballot, rather than a *straight-ticket* of one party.

4. **B**. The US has a moderate-to-low turnout rate compared to other countries. Presidential Election years bring out more voters than do other election years.

5. **D**. The House of Representatives is chosen by the people. A census taken every 10 years determines how many seats are up for grabs in each state. The Seventeenth Amendment of 1913 allowed for Senators to be chosen by the people. Today, the people still vote for *electors*, and not the President directly.

6. **D**. Christian fundamentalists would have opposing views compared to liberals who traditionally vote Democratic.

7. **A**. Political socialization is the study of how a young person develops their ideology. Overwhelmingly, young people tend to carry out their parents' beliefs. It's all about the dinner table.

8. **C**. A secret, or Australian ballot, was created as part of Progressive Era reforms c1900.

9. **C**. People with higher education levels tend to be more active in politics.

10. **E**. A traditionally conservative economic approach would be limiting the amount of government control over the economy. Conservatives are also for tax breaks which will channel more money into the economy.

Political Parties, Interest Groups, and the Media

Elections, political parties, interest groups, and the media are considered *linkage institutions*, or entities that bring the citizen closer to the political process. Political parties were never in the Constitution, but they naturally evolved over the course of American History. Today, there are two major parties, and an array of minor ones which look to bring issues into the spotlight.

But what influences political parties and public officials? In *Federalist #10*, Madison spoke of how factions could be kept in check. Today, there are too many factions to count, and they are more influential than ever. Though there are laws which govern their actions, special interest groups have a great say as to what policy is created.

Also influencing policy is the media. For decades, different forms of media have brought issues into living rooms. Today, news winds up on personal devices. Although the media is supposed to be objective, they sometimes take minor issues and escalate them into stories that dominate the headlines.

HERE IS WHAT YOU NEED TO KNOW:
• POLITICAL PARTIES
Definition: Political Party

A political party organizes and leads people who have the same interests. Their goal is to win elections and control government and policy. The two major parties in the United States are:

1. **Democrats** - tend to be more liberal, strong in blue states, mascot is the donkey.

2. **Republicans** - tend to be more conservative, strong in red states, mascot is the elephant.

People join parties for different reasons, including spreading ideology and serving the common good. Other people join for *solidary incentives*, such as the honor, fun, and the fellowship that politics brings them.

Question: In a nutshell, what is the history of American political parties?

Throughout the history of the US, there have been several *realignments*, or *critical periods*, where there were shifts in the political landscape, and a different political party began to dominate. Realignment can coincide with shifts in regional allegiance as well. You should know:

1. Originally, there were no political parties. George Washington warned about the dangers of them. In fact, political parties are not in the Constitution…as stated above, they are in the *unwritten constitution*.

2. The first political parties resulted from an argument over "strong government vs. states' rights." Followers of Alexander Hamilton (Federalists who wanted a stronger government) favored loose interpretation of the Constitution, and use of the Elastic Clause in creating the National Bank. Thomas Jefferson's supporters feared a strong government, favored strict interpretation, and became the Democratic-Republicans.

3. *Jacksonian Democracy* took place c1830, as the followers of Andrew Jackson believed that the "common man" should be involved in politics. His conservative adversaries, the Whigs, were opposed to Jackson's veto of the re-charter of the Bank of the United States.

3. The Democrats remained, but the modern-day Republicans came into being over the issue of slavery. Like the Whigs, the Republicans

were conservatives who supported big business.

4. Republicans dominated almost all Presidential Elections from 1860-1908. Geographically, from the Civil War until the 1960s, Democrats could always count on the "Solid South" for Electoral Votes. Meanwhile, the North was overwhelmingly Republican. However, this would change.

5. ***Franklin D. Roosevelt attracted more Democrats in the North as part of his New Deal Coalition.*** Liberals, African Americans, women, economists, and union leaders flocked to the party in the 1930s. The New Deal was a plan to get the United States out of the Great Depression with extensive public works programs (public jobs) and banking reform. This hands-on economic approach clashed greatly with traditional Republican values.

6. Civil Rights also altered the political landscape. Democrats Harry Truman and Lyndon Johnson's support for civil rights attracted many in the North to the Party. Since then, the Northern states have been more liberal on social issues.

7. Today, Republicans dominate the South and middle of the country, while Democrats are strongest in the Northeast and on the Pacific coast. Swing states, or those which are split pretty equally, include Florida, Ohio, Iowa, Colorado, and Nevada (as per the Election of 2012).

Development of US Political Parties

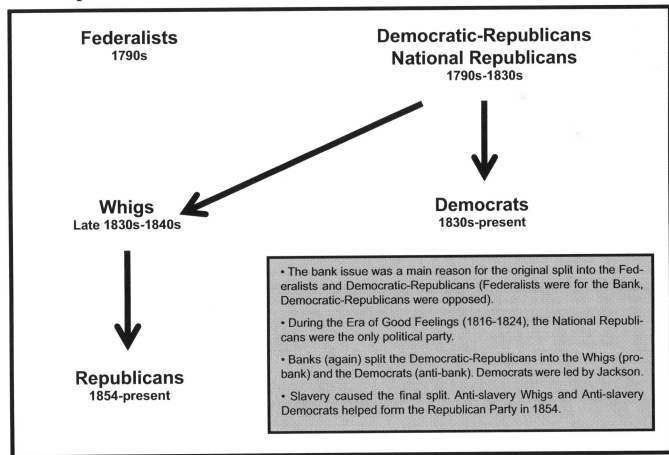

Question: What are Minor/Third Parties?

Over the history of the United States, there have been important *minor*, or *third parties*. With enough support, a third party can impact an election by:

1. Bringing new issues into play.
2. Taking away votes from another candidate, thereby changing the election's outcome. For instance, in 1912, Theodore Roosevelt's Bull Moose (Progressive) Party took votes away from incumbent President, Republican William H. Taft. Democrat Woodrow Wilson emerged as the victor. The strongest third party Presidential candidate in recent decades was Ross Perot in 1992, who received almost 19% of the vote against incumbent George H.W. Bush, and the election's winner Bill Clinton.

Other important minor parties to know are the Free-Soil party which wanted to stop the spread of slavery, the Populist Party of the 1890s which looked to protect farmers and expand political rights, the Prohibition Party which wanted to end the sale of alcohol, and in recent decades the Libertarian Party and the Green Party. These parties can be considered *ideological parties*, who rather than winning, are more concerned with conveying their views.

Minor parties have an uphill battle in Presidential Elections, as they are not usually invited to the debates. In addition, the winner-take-all format of the Electoral College (explained later), makes it less likely for them to win a state, and nearly impossible for them to capture the election.

Definition: Sponsored Party

Sometimes, a local political party is greatly controlled by an organization that has strong community ties. For example, if there was a large union-run steel plant in a town, it would likely fund the Democratic Party, and sponsor many of the candidates who run locally for office.

Question: How are today's political parties configured?

Every four years, a **national convention** takes place to nominate a Presidential candidate. As far as the party hierarchy:

1. The **national committee** is a large group of representatives from every state. They range from Congressional officials to local state politicians. These people elect the party's **national chairperson** who is in charge of raising money and promoting party interests. In state central committees, the party state chairperson would be elected.
2. There's also a congressional campaign committee which helps out those in the party who are running for office, or reelection.
3. Power trickles down to other local elections in counties, towns, and villages. It's in the party's greatest interest to win elections at every **precinct**, or voting district.

Question: How might candidates at the state level stray from the national party platform?

State and national political parties can differ. For example, in traditional blue (liberal Democrat) states such as New York and New Jersey, Republican leaders have supported liberal issues such as same-sex marriage and gun control. Locally, this can be advantageous. A Presidential candidate, however, would be less successful in deviating from the party platform.

Definition: Political Machine

This is a political party group that gains members and votes by offering money, jobs, or favors in return. William M. Tweed was the head of Tammany Hall, a machine in New York City where people "voted early and often" to support the Democratic Party. Tweed's "Ring" basically ran New York City in the 1870s, as members of the Democratic Party controlled all powerful offices there. Tammany Hall also helped immigrants find jobs in exchange for votes. New York was an oasis of **municipal** (city) **corruption**, as bribery and kickbacks were common.

Definition: Divided Government

Very often in US History, the Executive and Legislative Branches have been controlled by different political parties. The people can check the power of political parties by voting a divided government. However, division usually leads to less getting done, as partisanship has sometimes trumped service. Divided government can pose a challenge to Presidents hoping to get appointees approved. Sometimes the person appointed may not be the first choice…but the person who is most likely to get confirmed.

Oftentimes, the House of Representatives and the Senate are controlled by different parties as well. This leads to gridlock, or difficulty passing laws, as bills can be passed in the House, but not in the Senate.

In addition, *party polarization* often occurs. This is when most of one political party votes the opposite of the other party. This type of ideological division can make it hard to compromise on even moderate issues.

- **INTEREST GROUPS**

Definition: Interest Group

An *interest group* is an organization that tries to influence government, and get them to support a specific agenda. *Unlike a political party which has a wide range of objectives, special interest groups are usually concerned with only one or a few issues.*

One of the greatest influences of interest groups is raising money for campaigns. They give money to candidates who they believe will support their cause.

Interest groups can file lawsuits to support their agenda, and are involved in *lobbying*, or trying to persuade politicians to agree with them. The end goal is to have officials create or vote for policies that favor the interest group. *Direct lobbying* includes direct contact between the lobbyist and the lawmaker.

Lobbyists must be registered, obey campaign finance laws, have limits on gifts, and must disclose their financial activities in reports. They can lobby on behalf of people, groups, or corporations (called *corporate lobbyists*). Many lobbyists have offices on DC's K Street.

Lobbying laws requiring registration and reporting of financial activities were established by the **Federal Regulation of Lobbying Act** of 1946, and clarified by the **Lobbying Disclosure Act** of 1995.

It's important to know that lobbyists also help legislators by offering technical information on issues. They will provide specific plans to help presidents and members of Congress draw up policies.

Definition: Revolving Door

Sometimes private workers (some of who used to be lobbyists) leave their jobs to become public workers…or public workers join the private industry. This switch in jobs is called the *revolving door*, and could lead to corruption. What if a former government worker uses old contacts in Washington and starts lobbying for the private sector? Or, what if a new public worker starts to listen to old friends in the private world? These are both possibilities through the revolving door.

Definition: Grassroots lobbying/grassroots mobilization

Grassroots lobbying occurs when the general public tries to pressure politicians and affect the legislature. This can be done by using the media, phone call campaigns, and more prevalent today, social media on the internet. Such *mobilization* and public pressure can sway an official to vote a certain way, and gives average people a voice on issues. In addition, grassroots lobbying is far cheaper than direct lobbying. The NRA, NAACP, Sierra Club, and AARP have all used grassroots lobbying. Most recently, the Tea Party Movement has become a large voice in trying to reduce government spending. They have mobilized immensely online and in public demonstrations.

Question: What special interests have affected US History?

As James Madison predicted (in *Federalist #10*), factions were inevitable. Such factions, or special interests, have included: abolitionists, farmers of the Granger Movement in the late nineteenth century, and activists in *social movements* (movements that look to reshape the social culture). Important social movements in US History included prohibition, women's rights, and civil rights.

Question: What has happened to the number of interest groups over the last 60 years?

Answer: Since World War II, there has been an enormous increase in interest group activity. Most interest groups today have emerged since 1950. *Because of this new strength in interest groups, political parties have lost some of their power.*

Question: What are some special interest groups to know, and what do they support?

Answer: There are thousands of interest groups who look to influence opinion. Here are ten major ones:

1. **AARP** (American Association of Retired Persons) - looks to enhance the quality of life for people over the age of 50.

2. **ACLU** (American Civil Liberties Union) - defends liberty and the rights of all people.

3. **AFL-CIO** (The American Federation of Labor and Congress of Industrial Organizations) - Represents the workers of many unions such as the United Mine Workers of America and United Auto Workers, as well as trade unions (electricians, plumbers), teachers' unions, and law enforcement unions.

4. **AMA** (American Medical Association) - protects public health and looks out for the interests of physicians.

5. **American Farm Bureau Federation** - supports agricultural workers and their families.

6. **NAACP** (National Association for the Advancement of Colored People) - looks to foster civil rights and end discrimination.

7. **NAM** (National Association of Manufacturers) - represents manufacturers of all sizes.

8. **NRA** (National Rifle Association) - protects the right to bear arms, and encourages safety and training for those who use firearms.

9. **Tea Party Movement** - aims to lower taxes and reduce government spending.

10. **US Chamber of Commerce** - represents businesses of all sizes.

NOTE: Some issues, such as abortion, have interests on both sides, as seen with both the National Right to Life Committee and

NARAL Pro-Choice America.

Question: Which interest groups would focus on what agency?

Answer: Some interest groups might focus on multiple agencies, but to give you an idea of who they might influence:

NAM could target the Federal Trade Commission which regulates businesses.

NAACP and ACLU might contact the Department of Justice which makes sure that rights are not being violated.

Environmental groups could target the EPA (Environmental Protection Agency) which monitors pollution and the safety of the environment.

AARP might lobby the Social Security Administration.

Question: How do interest groups use the legal system to their advantage?

Interest groups use the legal system to support their agenda. Public-interest law firms bring lawsuits (*litigation*) on behalf of individuals. Lawsuits are a way of changing policy without going through legislatures. As will be discussed in the Judicial Branch chapter, strategies involve *amicus curiae* briefs ("friend of the court") and *class action suits*.

Definition: Public-interest group

This type of interest group looks to benefit all of society, and is not just focused on aiding a select few with a narrow issue. An example would be the Sierra Club, which promotes conservation and education about the environment.

Question: How do interest groups raise money?

Answer: Because interest groups spend a great deal of money on getting their word out, and often offer *incentives*, or enticing benefits for those who join, they need to raise capital. This can be done in the following ways:

1. Dues, especially for union groups.
2. Foundation grants - these are large sums of money that come from organizations or family funds set up by wealthy donors.
3. Federal grants - the government dishes out money to support some programs or projects run by interest groups.
4. Mailings and e-mailings are done with the hope of recruiting donors and members.

Question: How do interest groups impact elections?

Answer: Interest groups raise a ton of money in *campaign contributions* for candidates. This money is used for everything from leasing an office for volunteer staff, to buying airtime for commercials.

Having a large staff is important for aiding the *GOTV* (Get Out The Vote) movement. This is a means of getting potential supporters, who don't normally vote, to cast a ballot.

Definition: PACs

As stated, a major focus of interest groups is trying to help ally politicians get elected. A PAC is a *political action committee*, and it is used by groups such as businesses and labor unions to raise money for a candidate's election campaign. Though there are donation limits, PACs are of great influence on legislators, as politicians need immense sums of money to have a successful campaign.

It should be noted that most PACs are tax-exempt organizations known as 527s. If an interest group helps the social well-being (called a social welfare organization), and gives to a political campaign, they can be a 501(c)(4), where donors can be kept anonymous. The NAACP, AARP, and the ACLU are three such social welfare organizations.

Definition: Hard and Soft money used in campaigns

The Supreme Court has supported the right of PACs and individuals to give money to campaigns. The decision of **Buckley v. Valeo** (1976) stated that donations are a form of free speech protected by the First Amendment. The case also approved legal limits to contributions. However, issues regarding soft money continued to be debated.

But first ... Hard money refers to money given to a campaign within the legal limits set by the *Federal Election Commission*, which was established by Congress in 1974 to enforce the *Federal Election Campaign Act*. As of 2013, a regular person, or individual campaign donor, can give $2,600 to a candidate per election, while a PAC can give $5,000. Increases in the limits for what individuals can give will decrease the power of PACs.

However, more money *used* to be given in *soft money*. Instead of being given to candidates, *soft money could be donated in enormous amounts for political party activities*, such as getting out the vote ... which of course, indirectly helps out candidates anyway. Soft money was restricted by the Bipartisan Campaign Reform Act (explained next).

Definition: Bipartisan Campaign Reform Act of 2002

When the two parties work together on something, it's called *bi-partisan legislation*. Sometimes referred to as the McCain-Feingold Act, the *Bipartisan Campaign Reform Act* changed the way that campaigns can be financed. It restricted use of soft money that was given to the national party committee for federal campaigns. The act also made candidates "approve this message" on their ads.

Furthermore, the act restricted labor union and corporate sponsored advertisements in the days leading up to an election. This provision of the law was struck down by the Supreme Court in 2010, as the justices ruled in *Citizens United v. Federal Election Commission* that it was a violation of free speech.

Definition: Super PACs

Recently, the term Super PAC has been applied to what is known as an "independent expenditure." These organizations can spend as much money as they want, *so long as the money isn't directly connected to a candidate or political party*. Super PACs flood the airwaves with election commercials that try to convince people to vote a certain way. Many of their ads are negative. It's almost as if the candidates are paying for these commercials themselves... but they aren't. Indirectly, Super PACs help out both a candidate and a party.

• THE MASS MEDIA
Question: What forms of media are there?

The structure of the media has changed immensely over the last few decades. Here's a quick historic look at the media:

1. **Newspapers** - When the ratification of the Constitution was argued, Federalists and Anti-Federalists published their ideas in newspapers. This, of course, is where people got their news back then. Sometimes the papers were guilty of *yellow journalism*. In fueling sentiment in favor of the Spanish American War, William Randolph Hearst and Joseph Pulitzer provid-

ed inaccurate and sensational reporting to sell newspapers in the late nineteenth century.

2. **Magazines and books** - Political statements continued to be made in print. *Muckrakers* were journalists who dug up dirt on society and exposed their findings to the world. Muckraking was prevalent in the early twentieth century, and is given credit for making food safer to eat, and bringing down unfair monopolies.

3. **Radio** - In the 1920s, radio became popular, and it still has a strong presence today. Franklin D. Roosevelt utilized radio for his Fireside Chats, which calmed fears and informed the public during the Great Depression. Today, the President still gives a weekly radio address.

4. **Television** - Television was around in the 1950s, but in 1960 it might have determined the Presidential Election. John F. Kennedy and Richard M. Nixon were the first presidential candidates to debate on television. To those watching on TV, JFK came across as suave and charming. Many folks who listened on the radio thought Nixon was stronger. Today's national newscast and political talk shows are powerful in conveying information.

5. **Cable television** - Cable TV networks hit their stride in the 1990s. Today, a 24-hour news-cycle occurs, where the slightest misstep by a candidate gets incredible scrutiny. Both liberal and conservative talk shows can be found daily on cable.

6. **Internet** - Like cable, there's a 24-hour news-cycle on the internet, where events are updated instantly. In addition, all political ideologies and interest groups have webpages which outline their ideas and objectives.

Definition: Associated Press

The Associated Press is a not-for-profit news cooperative where news is gathered by thousands of journalists and shared by its members. Associated Press stories can be found on all outlets of media.

Question: How has the media changed?

Through the 1990s, the national network newscasts experienced remarkably high television ratings. Today, there are so many outlets that the national newscast, though still powerful, has lost some of its power. Although older audiences still watch the national newscast, younger ones are getting more of their news from the internet or off of social media.

As candidate and as President, Barack Obama used social media and the internet to cater to younger audiences. He announced to the world who his running-mate was via a text message (Joe Biden). The media can be of great opportunity to the President, as it can be a means of conveying and supporting the White House's agenda. *As leader of the country, the President commands the nation's audience with far more flair than Congress.*

The President often assembles the press to highlight achievements and future objectives. Though, sometimes the press becomes adversarial, or looks to use its power to expose or bring down a politician.

Definition: Press Secretary

The President appoints a press secretary whose job it is to meet with reporters and answer questions. The press secretary also aids the President before he or she is addressed by the media. Congressional members and high-ranking state officials also have press secretaries.

Question: How does the media report campaigns?

Today, the news never stops on a campaign.

In presidential elections, debates are televised to all markets (viewing areas) and each candidate is given equal time to speak. However, often the media downplays the issues and looks at the more entertaining polls and standings of the candidate's debate wins and losses. This is called *horse-race journalism*. In Presidential Campaigns, the media spends so much time on the candidate's life story, image, and gaffe sound-bites (mess-ups); they often overlook what's at stake.

Today, much mud-slinging takes place on commercials. These "attack-ads" look to destroy the integrity of the other candidate. Frequently, the talk-shows will feature negativity as often as they will positive investigations.

Definition: Watchdog Media

The media is a "watchdog," as it acts as a guardian against scandal, illegal activities, and undesirable situations. They do this for two reasons. First, scandals sell newspapers and get people to watch television. Second, they expose wrongdoing that infringes on the public good. Famously, reporters Bob Woodward and Carl Bernstein exposed Nixon's Watergate Scandal, where there was a cover-up of a break-in at the Democratic Party headquarters. As a watchdog, the media can also expose illegal activities of interest groups and corporations.

It's important to note, that with people locked into the news on television, radio, print, and personal devices, the media can actually control what issues are considered important. When different news agencies jump all over a story, it can inflate its importance … that is, until the next story comes along.

Question: How does the media affect public policy?

The media covers issues they hope people will find important and relevant. These issues tend to be the ones that can affect policy. Stories on gun violence, for example, often lead to the debate on gun control. Stories on medical costs drive the debate on health care.

Unfortunately, ***media bias*** comes into play, as various newspapers and television outlets can have different ideologies. In addition, much of what people know about candidates comes from the media, and therefore voting decisions are derived from what is seen on television or read in a newspaper. Thus, the people who make public policy can be elected with the help of the media.

Review Questions

1. Who of the following was NOT included in the New Deal Coalition?
   A) Minorities
   B) Blue collar workers
   C) Women
   D) Labor Unions
   E) Laissez-faire economists

2. Which of the following displays the greatest importance of third parties?
   A) Bringing to the forefront new issues that were rarely debated
   B) Giving candidates experience before they shift to a major party
   C) A large percentage of races are won by third parties
   D) Third parties have greater control over the media
   E) Minor parties are free from the impact of interest groups

3. What is the major objective of PACs?
   A) Lobbying Congress for amendments
   B) Regulating federal agencies
   C) Spending money on election campaigns
   D) Helping minor parties become major ones
   E) Getting Presidents to nominate favorable justices

4. An example of a public-interest group issue would be one that
   A) grants federal land to Native Americans
   B) promotes cleaner air
   C) lowers taxes on cigarettes
   D) raises the price of corn for farmers
   E) lowers tax rates for retired people

5. All of the following are legal actions of interest groups EXCEPT:
   A) Buying votes
   B) Campaign contributions
   C) Lobbying
   D) Litigation
   E) Presenting information

6. Which interest group looks to support the interests of doctors?
   A) NAACP
   B) AFL-CIO
   C) ACLU
   D) AMA
   E) NRA

7. The main purpose of grassroots lobbying is to
   A) bring attention to new candidates
   B) meet directly with politicians and sway their opinions
   C) provide campaign funds for candidates
   D) bring litigation into the court system
   E) persuade politicians to support certain policies

8. Critical realignments occur when
   A) Political parties gain strength in new areas
   B) Minority party candidates are elected
   C) Presidents capture the Electoral Vote but not the popular vote
   D) Women begin to outvote men
   E) The media backs a certain candidate for office

9. Who of the following can utilize the media to their greatest advantage?
   A) President
   B) Speaker of the House
   C) Majority Leader in Senate
   D) Governor of a state
   E) Vice President

10. Which statement about the media is true?
    A) The media will only be positive with regards to a sitting President
    B) The national newscasts are becoming less popular with younger generations
    C) The media always gives more attention to issues, than to polls, during a Presidential campaign
    D) Print media has expanded circulation in the last decade
    E) Politicians have been reluctant to use social media for campaigning

Free-Response Questions

I. Interest groups have an incredible impact on both political parties and how public policy is created.

    A. Identify two methods used by interest groups that affect the political process. Explain how each method can foster the ideas of the interest group. [pp. 31-33]

    B. Select two of the following groups and explain how they might use their influence to affect government. [pp. 32-33]
- National Association for the Advancement of Colored People (NAACP)
- Tea Party Movement
- National Rifle Association (NRA)
- American Association of Retired Persons (AARP)
- National Association of Manufacturers (NAM)

    C. Explain the main objective of PACs. Identify one limitation of campaign finance. [pp. 33-34]

II. Although the Constitution did not mention political parties, they have had a great influence on American government since the eighteenth century. Over the course of Untied States history, political parties have grown in strength, and have greatly affected the activities of the Legislative and Executive Branch.

    A. Identify what is meant by a critical period or realignment. Explain one specific realignment or critical period in American History. [p. 28]

    B. Explain how party polarization can hinder legislation. [p. 31]

    C. Describe one impact that minor parties can have on the political process. [p. 30]

    D. Identify one obstacle that hinders minor parties from becoming major ones. [p. 30]

Answers and Explanations

1. **E.** The New Deal was the opposite of laissez-faire, as there was immense government interaction with the economy.

2. **A.** Third parties, or minor parties, bring attention to issues. The Free-Soil Party highlighted slavery, while the Populist Party suggested new reforms that eventually became law years later.

3. **C.** PACs, or Political Action Committees, are formed as a means to give money to candidates for elections.

4. **B.** A public-interest group supports issues that benefit the general public. A cleaner air law would fit that category.

5. **A.** Although interest groups can give money to candidates, they can't legally buy a vote in Congress.

6. **D.** The American Medical Association looks out for people in the medical profession.

7. **E.** Grassroots lobbying occurs when the general public tries to pressure politicians and affect the legislature. This can be done by using the media, phone call campaigns, and more prevalent today, social media on the internet.

8. **A.** Realignments, or critical periods, occur when there are shifts in the political landscape and certain political parties dominate for years to come. It can coincide with changes as to how regions of the country vote.

9. **A.** The President commands the greatest audience, and can use the prestige of the office to convey the White House's agenda.

10. **B.** Younger generations get a lot of news from the internet, social media, and cable. Though still popular among older audiences, the national newscast used to be the only place to get the evening news.

The Legislative Branch

The Legislative Branch makes laws. That seems like a simple task, right? But procedures in Congress are quite complex. For a bill to become a law, much research, debate, and arm-twisting takes place. Although similar, there *are* differences between the House of Representatives and the Senate. Just because a bill seems popular in one chamber, doesn't necessarily mean it will become law. Between filibusters, logrolling, riders, and pork, what would seem like a simple task, has turned into a complex web of politics. Oh yeah, and that's before the bill even gets to the President's desk. Buckle your safety-belts for the inner-workings of the Legislative Branch.

HERE IS WHAT YOU NEED TO KNOW:

Question: What are the major powers of Congress (term commonly used when speaking of the House and the Senate)?

Answer: Congress can:

1. Lay and collect taxes - NOTE: *All revenue (money) bills __must__ start in the House.*
2. Borrow money
3. Declare war (and raise and support an army)
4. Regulate interstate commerce (trade between two or more states), and regulate commerce with foreign nations
5. Coin money
6. Fix the standard for weights and measures
7. Establish post offices
8. Change the size of the Supreme Court, and establish a court system below it

Question: Which House is closer to the people?

Answer: *The most important thing to remember is that the House of Representatives is the one that's tied to the people.* They represent small districts, as opposed to large states. That's why their term is short (so more elections can occur), the money bills start there, and it was the only office a citizen could vote for in 1789.

Question: What are the major party leadership positions of each house?

In the Senate, you need to know:

1. **President pro tempore** - Presides over the Senate (the Constitution states the Vice President is the President of the Senate, but rarely does so), and is selected by the majority party. Recently it's been the senior member of the majority party.

2. **Majority Leader** - Leader of the party that has a majority in the Senate.

3. **Majority Whip** - Helps to round up votes within the majority party.

4. **Minority Leader** - Leader of the party that does not have a majority.

5. **Minority Whip** - Helps to round up votes within the minority party.

6. **Party Conference Chairperson** - Each party has its own meeting, and designates a leader to preside over these closed-door sessions known as party conferences.

In the House, you need to know:

1. **Speaker of the House** - Elected by the House of Representatives, the Speaker presides over the House. Most likely, this person has been voted in by the majority party, and is therefore that party's leader.

2. Similar to the Senate, both the majority and minority parties have leaders and whips. NOTE: The House uses the term Democratic or Republican to describe the Minority Whip

(such as: *Democratic Whip*).

3. **Republican Conference Chair** - Heads the organization of all House Republicans.

4. **Democratic Caucus Chair** - Heads the organization of all House Democrats.

Definition: Impeachment

Impeachment does *not* mean to kick out of office! The House of Representatives can impeach certain federal officials for *treason, bribery, or other high crimes and misdemeanors*. Impeachment means to "charge with a crime." After the House impeaches, the Senate holds a trial and decides if the official is guilty. If found guilty, the official would then be removed from office. Two Presidents have been impeached (Andrew Johnson and Bill Clinton). Neither was convicted (found guilty), and thus was not removed from office.

Question: What are major differences between the House and the Senate?

1. The House has 435 members, and can initiate *revenue (money) bills* and begin impeachment proceedings. It chooses a President if no one wins the Electoral Vote. Bills are introduced in a "hopper" before being referred to a committee.

2. The Senate has 100 members, and can ratify treaties, approve presidential appointments, and hold a trial for the impeached official. The Senate has no limit on debate, as filibusters (explained later) can protect the minority party. The Senate is generally referred to as the *upper house*.

3. In terms of procedure, the Senate tends to be less formal than the House. After all, there are only 100 Senators compared to 435 Representatives. Not as many rules are needed in smaller settings.

4. Also important to know is that under the original Constitution, people did not vote for their Senators. The **Seventeenth Amendment** changed that in 1913.

Definition: Incumbent

Incumbents are those who currently hold an office. Holding that office helps immensely towards getting reelected, as voters are familiar with the name on the ballot, and the candidate may have helped develop programs that have benefited constituents. In addition, incumbents have greater success in campaign fundraising. Statistics show that incumbents are overwhelmingly reelected, though ***incumbency tends to help out Representatives a bit more than it does Senators***.

For members who are elected for the first time, they usually become popular rather quickly. This so-called ***sophomore surge*** will be apparent when comparing the difference between votes received in the first election, and the more impressive reelection.

Question: What is the difference between a marginal and safe district?

A marginal district is one where there are tight elections. Safe districts are those where the incumbent will overwhelmingly win.

Definition: Franking Privilege

Members of Congress have benefits such as salaries and health plans, but they are also allowed to use generous amounts of stationery and postage to communicate with constituents. This so-called "communication" usually turns into "campaigning," as incumbents send out millions of mailings around campaign time. All of this is paid for with taxpayer dollars. This postage perk is called the ***franking privilege***.

Question: What trends have occurred in Congress?

Like other areas of government, more women and minorities have secured seats over the last few decades.

From the days of Franklin D. Roosevelt (1930s) until the mid-1990s, Democrats often dominated the House, and sometimes had control of the Senate at the same time. Since the 1990s, Republicans have surged to capture the House during most of the two-year sessions.

Definition: Committee and Chairs

Legislators are assigned to *committees*, which research specific aspects of potential legislation. This *specialization* allows them to become experts regarding certain policies. Within these committees, legislators evaluate information, and make recommendations to the legislature. Committees also oversee the agencies of the Executive Branch, and if necessary, can conduct investigations.

Traditionally, the *chairperson*, or leader of the committee, is the majority party representative with the most *seniority*, or longest term of service. However, a secret ballot is used, and in 1995, the House established a six-year term limit on chairs (the Senate later followed as well). A member can only serve as a chair on one committee. Chairs used to pull more weight when they were appointed based on party loyalty.

Question: What types of Congressional committees should I know about?

1. **Standing committees** - Permanent groups that oversee the bills that deal with specific types of issues. Nearly all standing committees have *subcommittees* which are even more specialized in what they research and analyze.

2. **Select/Special committees** - These are usually temporary committees which study a specific issue before reporting back to the House or Senate. They usually work on issues that are suddenly of great public interest, such as Global Warming.

3. **Joint committees** - These are comprised of House and Senate members of both parties. They relay their research back to their respective Houses.

4. **Conference Committee** - These are temporary committees who look to find compromises regarding different versions of the same bill that has passed both the House and Senate.

Question: What specific standing committees are most important to know?

Answer: Both houses have similar standing committees. The House has more, as they are a larger entity. You should know:

1. **Ways and Means (House)** - They recommend how to raise money through measures such as taxes and tariffs. Their subcommittees also oversee Medicare, unemployment benefits, and Social Security.

2. **Rules (House)** - The Traffic Cop of Congress," they determine under what rules bills come to the floor. They also put bills on the House calendar.

3. **Appropriations (House and Senate)** - They determine how the government spends its money.

4. **Foreign Relations (Senate)/Foreign Affairs (House)** - They oversee foreign policy. In terms of foreign policy, the Senate has more power, as it approves Presidential appointments and ratifies treaties.

Other standing committees found in both houses include Agriculture, Armed Services, Budget, and those dealing with Homeland Security and Energy.

Question: What are some rules established by The House Rules Committee?

A *closed rule* means there's a limit on debate, and a refusal to introduce amendments. An *open rule* allows amendments. A *restrictive rule* allows some, but not other amendments. The House can enforce a *germaneness requirement* as well, where proposed amendments must be relevant.

Definition: Bill

A bill is a proposal for a law. Most bills die. *Private bills* are those that deal with specific individuals or places. *Public bills* are those that apply to general issues and everyone in the nation.

Question: How does a bill become a law?

Answer: *9 magic words - Passed by House, Passed by Senate, Signed by President.*

Now more in depth: For business to be conducted, there must be a *quorum* (which according to the Constitution is a majority in each house, though the House only needs 100 in their Committee of the Whole to conduct business). A *roll call* of attendance confirms a quorum.

In the House, the bill is introduced by any member and placed in a box called a *hopper*. It then gets referred to a House committee. The House sub-committee is a subdivision of this committee, and it reports back to the full committee with revisions. If the bill survives, the *Rules Committee* then decides how, and at what speed, the bill will be considered by the House. Calendars list the bills that are being considered.

As stated earlier, a *closed rule* means the bill cannot be changed. An open rule allows amendments. A *restrictive rule* allows for certain, but not all, changes to occur. The bill then goes to the floor and is debated, and voted on.

In the Senate, the bill is introduced, and is similarly referred to a committee and subcommittee before being debated and voted on.

When a bill passes *with a simple majority* in one House, it goes to the other one to be considered.

If the bill passes in both the House and the Senate, it goes to the President's desk. NOTE: Sometimes, a *conference committee* negotiates the differences that might exist between the House and Senate versions of the bill. Their compromise is sent back to each chamber for one last approval.

The approved bill can either be signed by the President, or vetoed (struck down). If it is vetoed, then Congress can override this decree with a 2/3 override vote. Vetoes are not the norm, and an override of a veto rarely takes place.

Question: What else should I know about the veto?

Answer: A veto kills the entire bill. Even if the President doesn't like one sentence, if vetoed, the entire thing dies. Many state governors have what's called a *line-item veto*, which lets them pick and choose what they want to sign into law. The President does not have that luxury, though President Bill Clinton enjoyed a line-item veto for a short time before the Judicial Branch struck down the *Line Item Veto Act of 1996*.

Another type of veto to know is called the *pocket veto*. If the President does not sign the bill within 10 days, and Congress has *adjourned* (postpones meeting to another time), the bill dies. On the other hand, if the President doesn't act (neither signs nor vetoes) for

How a Bill Becomes a Law (Simplified)

Most bills can begin in either the House of Representatives or the Senate, with the exception of revenue (money) bills, which must begin in the House. Once approved in one House, it goes to the other. *In this example, a hypothetical bill will begin in the House.*

A. HOUSE OF REPRESENTATIVES

HOUSE COMMITTEE — A bill gets referred to a House committee. The smaller sub-committee reports back to the full committee with revisions.

HOUSE RULES COMMITTEE — Powerful committee that decides how a bill will be considered. It will also decide how amendments to the bill will take place.

FLOOR OF THE HOUSE — Bill is debated; the House votes. House can approve or kill the bill. Approved bill goes to Senate (Step B).

B. SENATE

SENATE COMMITTEE — Sub-committee and standing committee research, analyze, and construct the bill.

FLOOR OF THE SENATE — Bill is debated. Amendments may be added. The Senate votes and can approve or kill the bill.

C. CONFERENCE COMMITTEE

If there are differences between the House and Senate versions of the bill, a Conference Committee, made up of members of the House and Senate, will meet to work out the differences. The new bill they agree on must now be voted on by the House and the Senate. No more changes are allowed.

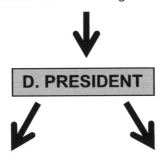

D. PRESIDENT

If the President signs. The bill becomes law.

If the President vetoes. The bill goes back to each house of Congress. If the House and the Senate vote for it again by a 2/3 vote, it becomes law. This is overriding a President's veto. If they don't get the 2/3 in each house, the bill is killed.

NOTE: If the President takes no action, and the bill sits on the President's desk for 10 days while Congress is in session, the bill becomes law. If Congress goes out of session before the 10 days are up, the bill is killed (Pocket Veto).

10 days, and Congress is in session, the bill becomes law without a signature.

Question: How often does a bill become a law?

Not often! That's important to know. Only very small percentages are signed into law.

Definition: Simple, Concurrent, and Joint Resolutions

Besides bills, Congress can pass resolutions which express positions, or are statements that affect inner operations. *Simple resolutions* affect only one house and don't have to be signed by the President because they are not binding laws.

Concurrent resolutions express sentiments or affect actions in both Houses, and don't need to be signed by the President.

Joint resolutions need approval of both houses, and carry the weight of law. They have to be signed by the President. Joint resolutions are also used to propose amendments, but those are sent to the states for ratification instead of the President.

Definition: Legislative veto

Declared unconstitutional in 1983, the ***legislative veto*** gave Congress the power to put provisions into laws which allowed them to negate some decisions made by the Executive Branch. In essence, this gave the Legislative Branch veto power over executive decisions. But it's no longer on the books.

Definition: Filibuster

In the Senate only, there's no limit to the length of debate. Because of this, if one party knows they are going to lose a vote, ***they try to delay the measure as long as possible***. Yes, if you are a Senator, you could read a telephone book aloud, and it can be considered debate. If 3/5, or 60, of the 100 Senators want the filibuster to end, they can vote for what's called ***cloture***.

Before a filibuster, a Senator might put a ***hold*** on a bill in an attempt to prevent it from reaching the floor. Though the Majority Leader can look beyond that hold, a filibuster will often follow.

Converse to filibusters, there could be ***unanimous consent agreements***, which sets the terms for the Senate's consideration of bills. Such terms could mean a lack of amendments to a bill, or a limit on debate. Unlike filibusters, these agreements save time in the legislative process.

Question: What strategies are often used to pass bills?

Answer: Congress can use one of the following tactics:

1. **Rider** - An added provision that might have nothing to do with the intent of the original bill. If the bill is popular, the rider will easily pass. When a bill has a lot of riders in it, it's known as a *Christmas tree bill*.

2. **Logrolling** - Supporting another politician's projects, so long as that politician shows mutual support. In other words, "if you vote for my bill, I'll vote for yours." This often speeds up the legislative process and allows Congress to pass more bills. NOTE: You should know that the word ***reciprocity*** (doing favors) can be associated with logrolling.

3. **Pork-barrel legislation** - Pork benefits only certain districts, usually in the form of public works projects such as bridges or roads. The idea is to bring money into certain areas and benefit specific representatives.

4. **Earmark** - This refers to when a part of

a spending bill allocates money for something specific. For example, if Congress allocated money in its budget to go directly to bridge construction in California, or a museum exhibit in Florida, those would be earmarks.

Definition: Congressional Caucus

When Congressional legislators band together to represent a certain ideology or interest, it's called a caucus. Caucuses can have a similar cultural background such as African American or Hispanic American. Sometimes bipartisan caucuses (both parties) will represent agendas of certain interest groups. Often, supporters of different ideologies within the party (liberal and conservative Democrats) will caucus together. NOTE: For the term caucus relevant for Presidential Elections, see the Executive Branch Chapter.

Definition: Congressional Reapportionment

Every ten years, a *census*, or detailed population count, is taken. Once the populations of the states are known, the number of representatives (in the House) each state has can be determined. So, if the population in your home state increases, you just might get more representatives. If it goes down, then the opposite could occur. And of course, the more representatives a state has, the greater its influence in Congress. Also, populous states will have more Electoral Votes at play. However, this could all change by the next census.

NOTE: The Senate is not affected, as each state always has two, no matter what happens to the population.

Definition: Gerrymandering and District Lines

Gerrymandering is the re-drawing of Congressional districts to aid the party in power of the state legislature, which draws the lines. It was first used by Massachusetts governor Elbridge Gerry in the early 1800s. In addition to Congressional districts, others such as school districts can also be gerrymandered by the group in power. Gerrymandering often solidifies incumbents in place, and can even be done as a political reward to prospective representatives. See the illustration on page 48.

Definition: *Baker* v. *Carr*, 1962

Despite gerrymandering, there are still rules that must be followed when drawing district lines.

Charles Baker lived in Tennessee. He believed the state was overdue for redrawing legislative district lines, and their lack of action was in violation of the state constitution. Baker wanted a greater number of districts in urban areas, where more people lived. Because he believed his vote counted less, he thought his **equal protection rights of the Fourteenth Amendment** were being violated. The Supreme Court agreed, and stated that the federal courts could hear cases and force states to redraw their district lines.

Also of note is *Wesberry* v. *Sanders* (1964), where the Supreme Court ruled that districts had to be of similar populations, adhering to the principle of "one person, one vote." In addition, *Reynolds* v. *Sims* (1964) proclaimed that state legislative districts must be proportioned equally, as per the equal protection clause of the Fourteenth Amendment.

The Supreme Court has also said that districts can't be racially drawn to decrease the impact of minority voters. Still, there are many *majority-minority districts*, or districts where the majority of the constituents are mi-

How does Gerrymandering Work?

OK...this is a little far-fetched. But here's how Gerrymandering works.

Wycliffe is a very large city in a populous northeastern state. It is so large, that the city contains 5 Congressional (House of Representatives) districts.

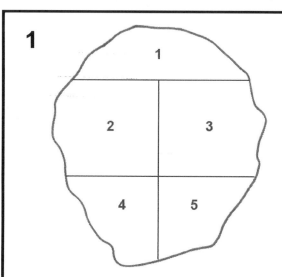

The Democratic-controlled state legislature drew the Congressional district boundaries with "normal" lines.

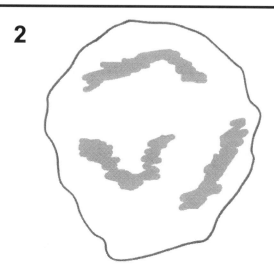

A recent survey shows where Republican voters and Democratic voters live in the city. Republican areas are shaded in grey. Democratic areas are white. There are obviously many more Democrats in Wycliffe than Republicans.

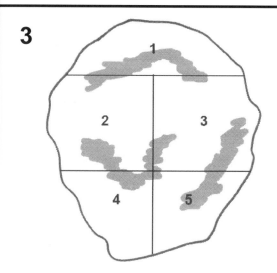

It's easy to see that Democrats outnumber Republicans in each district. Therefore, 5 Democrats will likely represent the state from Wycliffe in the House of Representatives.

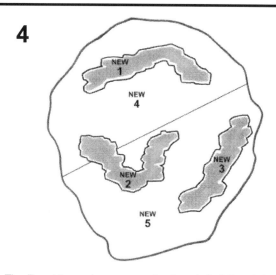

The Republicans have now gained control of the state legislature, and they want to change the boundaries of Wycliffe's 5 Congressional districts. By gerrymandering the boundaries, the Republicans will now have 3 seats, and the Democrats 2.

norities such as African Americans or Hispanic Americans.

Definition: Staff Agencies

Staff agencies are independent, and nonpartisan employees who work with Congress to make sure the federal government is doing its job properly. Three to know are:

1. **Congressional Budget Office** (CBO) - Provides economic data for Congress concerning spending and costs.

2. **General Accounting Office** (GAO) - Investigates how the federal government spends taxpayer money.

3. **Congressional Research Service** (CRS) - A part of the Library of Congress (the government's book, media, and copyright headquarters), the CRS provides policy and legal analysis to committees and members of Congress.

Definitions: Initiative, Referendum, Recall

In certain states, the *people* can have a big say in legislation. Each of these began during the Progressive Era of the early 1900s.

1. **Initiative** - Some states allow people to introduce bills directly into the state legislature.

2. **Referendum** - Some states allow people to vote on certain bills.

3. **Recall** - Some states allow voters to petition to remove incumbents from office prematurely. In these cases, there would be a special election to determine if the official stays or is replaced.

Review Questions

1. Which of the following is NOT a power of Congress?
   A) Declaration of war
   B) Regulation of interstate commerce
   C) Creation of the Postal Service
   D) Regulation of weights and measures
   E) Appointment of judges

2. Which of the following is a power of the House of Representatives?
   A) Filibuster
   B) Trying impeached officials
   C) Initiating revenue bills
   D) Confirming Supreme Court appointments
   E) Ratifying treaties

3. Which is true of the line-item veto for state governors?
   A) It allows them to veto a bill without an explanation
   B) Governors can veto tax bills a year before the budget is due
   C) If the legislature is not in session for ten days, a bill automatically becomes a veto
   D) Governors can veto portions of bills, but keep other parts
   E) A vetoed bill can't be altered and passed again by the legislature

4. Which of the following committees influences how money is generated from taxes and tariffs?
   A) Ways and Means
   B) Appropriations
   C) Rules
   D) Foreign Relations
   E) Budget

5. Which of the following legislative techniques is most associated with reciprocity, or the sharing of favors?
   A) Logrolling
   B) Rider
   C) Pork-barrel legislation
   D) Earmark
   E) Gerrymandering

6. Why is the census extremely important?
   A) It determines how many Senators each state has
   B) It increases the number of majority-minority districts
   C) It can bring cloture to a filibuster
   D) It is necessary for overriding a veto
   E) It determines reapportionment in the House of Representatives

7. Which of the following committees of Congress is considered permanent?
   A) Joint
   B) Conference
   C) Special
   D) Standing
   E) Rules

8. What did the Supreme Court decide in *Baker* v. *Carr*?
   A) All gerrymandering was unconstitutional
   B) A census must be taken every ten years
   C) The case of *Wesberry* v. *Sanders* was overturned
   D) Gerrymandering was acceptable if done so for racial purposes
   E) Federal courts can force states to redraw their district lines

9. Which of the following is true about how a bill becomes a law?
   A) Most bills become laws
   B) Congress often overrides vetoes
   C) If the president doesn't sign a bill, it can become a law anyway
   D) There can be unlimited debate in the House
   E) Conference committees can only be used for revenue bills

10. Which statement is true about incumbents?
    A) Incumbents are typically more popular in their first term
    B) Incumbency benefits a Representative more than it does a Senator
    C) Incumbents are less likely to use the franking privilege
    D) An incumbent is less likely to be a committee chair
    E) Incumbents can't be voted out of office after their second term

Free-Response Questions

I. Because there are so many jobs that need to be done, Congress has set up a system of committees where bills can be constructed and analyzed.
   A. Describe how specialization has become a part of the legislative process. [p. 43]
   B. Explain the purpose of two of the following committees. [p. 43]
      • Ways and Means
      • Appropriations
      • Rules
   C. In addition to laws, Congress can also pass resolutions. Explain two different types of resolutions, and indicate the role the President has, if any, in approving them. [p. 46]

II. The process for a bill to become a law is a complex one that involves many techniques and methods. Still, most bills are left dead on the floor of both houses.
   A. Identify two of the following, and explain their purpose in the law-making process.
      • Quorum [p. 44]
      • Veto [p. 44]
      • Standing Committee [p. 43]
   B. Explain two of the following techniques. Identify how they either help or hinder the passage of legislation. [p. 46]
      • Filibuster
      • Logrolling
      • Pork-barrel legislation
   C. Describe two differences between the House of Representatives and the Senate regarding two of the following. [p. 42]
      • Revenue bills
      • Impeachment proceedings
      • Legislative procedures

Answers and Explanations

1. **E**. The President in the Executive Branch appoints justices.

2. **C**. The House is closest to the people. Therefore, it has the shortest term (2 years), and starts the revenue (money) bills.

3. **D**. A line-item veto allows governors to veto only the unwanted portions of a bill.

4. **A**. The Ways and Means Committee recommends how to raise money through measures such as taxes and tariffs. Its subcommittees also oversee Medicare, unemployment benefits, and Social Security.

5. **A**. Logrolling is supporting another politician's projects, so long as that politician shows mutual support. This often speeds up the legislative process and allows Congress to pass more bills.

6. **E**. A census is a detailed population count which determines reapportionment, or the number of representatives a state has.

7. **D**. Standing committees are the permanent and most major committees of Congress. They are where most of the work gets done.

8. **E**. Because he believed his vote counted less, Baker thought his equal protection rights of the Fourteenth Amendment were being violated. The Supreme Court agreed, and stated that the federal courts could hear cases and force states to redraw their district lines.

9. **C**. If Congress remains in session for 10 days, the bill becomes law without the President's signature. If the President does not sign the bill within 10 days, and Congress has adjourned (postpones meeting to another time), the bill doesn't become a law. This is called a pocket veto.

10. **B**. Statistics show that Representatives have a slight edge over Senators when it comes to the benefits of being an incumbent. Representatives are also reelected every 2 years, as opposed to Senators which have 6 years in office per term.

The Executive Branch

The most high-profile office in all of the land is the Presidency of the United States. This can be a great job when times are good. But in times of crisis, this can be an unenviable position. Becoming the President is a three-stage process that begins about a year before the general election. Once elected, the President serves as Commander-in-Chief, signs or vetoes legislation, and appoints people to an array of offices. The Executive Branch's main job is to enforce the nation's laws. The President does this with the aid of the cabinet, the White House Staff, and a network of agencies within the Executive Branch.

HERE IS WHAT YOU NEED TO KNOW:

Question: How does a President win an election?

For the path to the Presidency just remember that **P**encils **N**eed **E**rasers…**P**rimary + **N**ominating Convention + **E**lectoral College.

Direct Primaries are small elections in the first half of the year that determine which candidate from each political party will be chosen at the ***nominating (national) convention***. The candidates nominated will then run in the November Presidential Election. NOTE: In some states, caucuses are held during primary season. In a ***caucus***, small meetings take place and people openly vote for state delegates who will represent candidates at the nominating convention. The first caucus of the season has recently been in Iowa, and has received great media attention.

Before there were primaries and nominating conventions, party bosses chose the candidates in their own caucuses (political meetings). By the 1830s, nominating conventions were established so that people could have a voice. ***Both primaries and nominating conventions have increased democracy and weakened the party leaders' control over election outcomes.***

Definition: Open and Closed Primary

In an ***open primary***, people can show up to the polling place and vote in one party's direct primary. In a ***closed primary***, only registered party members can vote. For example, Republicans would only be voting for Republicans.

Question: How do candidates campaign differently in the primary as opposed to the general election?

Answer: Candidates usually operate very differently. First, in the primaries, they are running against people of the same political party, and therefore they might have similar ideas. Also, the electorate usually supports most of the platform. It's in the November election that candidates must appeal to the general public. They often become more moderate in their demeanor.

Question: What should I know about the Presidential nominating (national) convention?

Today's nominating convention doesn't have much suspense. We almost always know who is being nominated based upon the outcome of the primary season. But, if there is no clear-cut frontrunner after the primaries, prepare for a great show! The convention could produce shocking surprises. Mostly though, today's conventions are a one-sided celebration that usually gives a short boost to each party in the polls. You also need to know:

1. Each party has their national convention at a site determined by the party leaders. They

choose how many delegates, or representatives, each state will have at the convention. Each party has their own method for doing this.

2. Over the last several decades, there has been an increase in both minority and female delegates at the conventions.

3. The primary elections determine how many delegates each candidate has in the bag at the convention. Though most of the delegates sent from the states pledge to support one candidate, some are unpledged. So too are the *superdelegates*, which are party leaders and elected officials who also attend the convention. They can support whoever they want, and have immense power at the convention.

4. The party also comes up with a *platform*, which are its positions on major issues.

5. The President and Vice Presidential candidates are announced on the same *ticket*. They appear together on the ballot, and have done so since the *Twelfth Amendment* (1804).

It should be noted that Presidential campaigns can apply for public funding for valid expenses. National political parties also receive some federal money for nominating conventions.

Definition: Electoral College

On Election Day, in all 50 states and the District of Columbia, people vote for *electors* who have sworn to vote for a candidate. People do NOT vote for the President directly. The number of Electoral Votes a state has is equal to the number of Representatives plus two, for the two Senators each state has.

Whoever gets a majority of votes in the *Electoral College* wins the November Election. The popular vote is irrelevant, and candidates therefore campaign in "swing states," or those states where the election can go either way. Typical blue (Democrat) and red (Republican) states don't see much campaigning, as the election results are rarely in doubt.

Whoever gets a *plurality* of votes (the most) in each state, gets ALL of that state's electoral votes. This is a *winner-take-all* scenario, which therefore makes it very hard for a third party to win the entire election. Plurality elections happen at all levels of government.

You need to know that to win a Presidential Election, a candidate must receive a majority of all possible Electoral Votes. If no candidate gets a majority, then the House of Representatives chooses the President.

Today, there are 538 electoral votes up for grabs. That's 435 Representatives + 100 Senators + 3 votes from Washington, DC (as per the Twenty-Third Amendment). Because they are the most populous states, California, Texas, New York, and Florida have the most electoral votes on the table.

At the end of the night, all of the secured Electoral Votes are added up. Whoever reaches 270 votes (which is a majority of the 538 possible votes), wins the election. The winner will be sworn into office on Inauguration Day (January 20th of the following year).

Critics of the Electoral College point out that in 1824, 1876, 1888, and 2000, a candidate won the popular vote, but lost the Electoral Vote. To get rid of the Electoral College, an amendment would have to be passed, which isn't very likely.

Question: What importance does a Vice Presidential candidate have?

It's always important to have a strong VP candidate, as he or she would take office if the President dies or becomes incapacitated, is removed from office, or has resigned. Vice

Presidents are often chosen to *balance a ticket*. In other words, if the Presidential candidate is very conservative, a more moderate VP can attract voters who are close to the middle of the political spectrum. Similarly, candidates often choose a VP who is from a different part of the country than they are. A popular VP candidate from a swing state can turn an election.

Question: What are the major powers of the President?

The President:

1. Is Commander-in-Chief of the military, and can use its might for defense and to enforce legislation
2. Signs and vetoes laws
3. Grants pardons (forgiveness with no penalty) or reprieves (penalty postponements) in federal cases
4. Makes treaties with foreign nations (which must be approved by 2/3 of the Senate)
5. Appoints government officials (which must be confirmed by a majority of the Senate)6. Recommends laws to Congress
7. Delivers the State of the Union Address
8. Can call Congress into a special session
9. Receives ambassadors

NOTE: These are called *formal powers*, as they are described directly in the Constitution. The President's *informal* powers would include things not exactly defined in the Constitution, such as executive orders and executive privilege (both explained later). Also, the President can set informal precedents, such as George Washington running for two terms. NOTE: The *Twenty-Second Amendment* limits the Presidency to two terms.

Definition: Executive Order

Especially in times of emergency, the President can issue an executive order, or a rule that holds the same weight as a law. Executive orders were instrumental in desegregating the military (under Harry Truman) and integrating schools (under Dwight Eisenhower).

Japanese internment during World War II gives a good look at checks and balances regarding an executive order. In 1942, President Franklin D. Roosevelt issued Executive Order 9066, which authorized the creation of military zones which excluded Japanese Americans. Congress then passed Public Law 503 making it a federal offense to violate the executive order, and many Japanese Americans were placed in internment camps. The Supreme Court later declared that internment was constitutional in the court case *Korematsu* v. *US*, as in times of war, such drastic measures could be taken.

Definition: War Powers Act (Resolution), 1973

However, an executive order doesn't mean the President can have unlimited power as Commander-in-Chief. After the Vietnam War, the *War Powers Act* was passed, stating that the President can't use extensive overseas force (for more than 60 days, followed by a 30-day withdrawal period) without the consent of Congress. In addition, Congress must be consulted at least 48 hours before the military is deployed.

Remember: *Congress declares war, not the President*. However, Korea and Vietnam were both undeclared wars. Today, a lengthy military operation can't be carried out without the backing of Congress. Twenty-first century operations in Afghanistan and Iraq both had their consent. The President must also rely on Congress to fund military operations. In addition, don't forget that the Senate confirms some military appointments, and ratifies treaties.

Definition: Cabinet

The cabinet exists to advise the president. Departments were created by Congress. Cabinet appointees must be approved by the Senate. Departments contain ***thousands of employees that make up a large bureaucracy*** (explained in depth later). A cabinet member's loyalty can sometimes be torn between the President and the Department. Important cabinet positions include:

1. **Secretary of State** - Deals with foreign affairs.

2. **Secretary of the Treasury** - Works with economic, tax, and financial issues.

3. **Secretary of Defense** - Protects the security of the American people. The government's top military advisors are called the Joint Chiefs of Staff.

4. **Attorney General of the Department of Justice** - Makes sure there is adequate protection of citizen rights in terms of criminal activity, and consumer exploitation.

5. **Secretary of the Interior** - Protects natural resources, including National Parks, and honors culture and Native American tribal communities.

Other departments include Agriculture, Commerce, Labor, Health and Human Services, Housing and Urban Development, Transportation, Energy, Education, Veterans Affairs, and Homeland Security.

Definition: White House Staff

In addition to the Cabinet, the President has a network of aides and advisors who *don't* need to be approved by the Senate. They typically work in the West Wing of the White House. The supervisor of these advisors is called the *Chief of Staff*. His or her assistant is called the Deputy Chief of Staff. They oversee the Executive Office of the President (EOP).

Definition: Executive Office of the President (EOP)

Today's White House Staff was created in the days of Franklin D. Roosevelt. Overseen by the White House Chief of Staff, the EOP is a series of federal agencies and advisors who help the President. Unlike the Chief of Staff, leaders of the EOP are appointed and confirmed by the Senate. Some of these federal agencies include the National Security Council (military and foreign policy advice), the Office of National Drug Control Policy, and the Office of Management and Budget. The latter is the largest office, and helps the President prepare the budget.

Other federal agencies assist in operations such as running the space program and protecting the forests. Some of the EOP positions have the status of Cabinet-rank. See the graphic on page 58 to better understand the composition of the Executive Branch.

Question: How is the White House Staff organized?

In one of three ways:

1. Pyramid structure - each assistant reports through their boss up to the Chief of Staff.

2. Circular structure - assistants report directly to the President.

3. Ad hoc structure - task forces, committees, special advisors, and informal groups report directly to the President.

Definition: Independent Regulatory Agency

Not in a cabinet department, there are independent agencies within the government. Some

The Executive Branch

The President
White House Staff
Chief of Staff
Deputy Chiefs of Staff
Counselor to the President
Senior Advisors

Executive Office of the President
Council of Economic Advisors
Council on Environmental Quality
Executive Residence
National Security Staff
Office of Administration
Office of Management & Budget
Office of National Drug Control Policy
Office of Science & Technology Policy
Office of the US Trade Representative
Office of the Vice President
White House Office

The Cabinet
Department of State
Department of the Treasury
Department of Defense
Department of Justice
Department of the Interior
Department of Agriculture
Department of Commerce
Department of Labor
Department of Health & Human Services
Department of Housing & Urban Dev.
Department of Transportation
Department of Energy
Department of Education
Department of Veterans Affairs
Department of Homeland Security

Important Independent Agencies include Federal Trade Commission, Central Intelligence Agency, Environmental Protection Agency, Federal Election Commission, Federal Communications Commission, and Federal Reserve Board.

of these independent agencies are ***set up by Congress to regulate specific industries***. For example, the FCC (Federal Communications Commission) monitors broadcast material on television and the radio. The FTC (Federal Trade Commission) makes sure that consumers are protected from unfair business decisions. The SEC (Security and Exchange Commission) protects investors and punishes those who illegally trade stocks and bonds.

Although the President appoints the board members of these agencies, they are difficult to remove from office (compared to cabinet members). Members also serve fixed terms and have some independence from the President.

The opposite of regulation would be ***deregulation***, which would be the process for which the government stops restricting activities (especially business ones).

In 1887, the first regulatory agency created was the Interstate Commerce Commission (ICC). It was established to regulate the abuses of the railroad industry.

Definition: Federal Reserve Board

The Federal Reserve System (The Fed) is also independent, and acts as the nation's central bank. The Federal Reserve Board monitors bank interest rates and how the US dollar is circulated.

Some believe the Fed is just as powerful as a cabinet department, because by controlling interest rates, they influence price inflation and deflation. With such power, it's no wonder why they are independent. We'll look more at their actions regarding monetary policy in the public policy chapter.

Question: How could the EOP work with other Agencies?

Answer: Let's say there was a security threat in the United States. The President can consult the head of the National Security Council (in the EOP), and the Central Intelligence Agency (CIA) director (outside of EOP). If inflation is an issue, the President can talk to the Council of Economic Advisors (EOP), as well as the Federal Reserve Board (outside of EOP). If there's an environmental calamity, both the Council on Environmental Quality (EOP) and the Environmental Protection Agency (outside EOP) can help.

Definition: Legislative Oversight

Although they are part of the Executive Branch, federal agencies and their policies are monitored by the Legislative Branch. If Congress believes bad decisions are being made, or mistakes have occurred, they can step in and hold people accountable for missteps. The main purpose of legislative oversight is to make sure that government workers are doing what they are supposed to be doing.

Definition: Advice and Consent

In Article II of the Constitution, it says the President should seek the advice of the Senate before nominating federal judges or making treaties. We know that the Senate must approve both, but it's important to note that by seeking advice and input, the President can avoid a controversial appointee and a potential embarrassing failure.

Definition: Executive Privilege

Conversations in the White House are confidential. To protect against publicizing classified items, the President, and other high-ranking Executive Branch workers, can refuse to hand over some information to Congress or any court. This is called executive privilege.

However, this does not work under all circumstances. In ***US v. Nixon*** (1974), the Supreme Court ordered President Richard Nixon to release the notorious tapes and documents relevant to the Watergate Scandal, where his administration covered up a break-in at the

Democratic offices in the Watergate Hotel. Executive privilege was not designed to shelter criminal activity.

Nixon remains the only President to resign the office.

Question: Can you please simplify the history of the Presidency?

Yes. George Washington was the first President, and he set certain precedents, or trends. He assembled the first cabinet, gave a farewell address, and only stayed in power for two terms. All Presidents followed suit, for the exception of Franklin D. Roosevelt, who was elected four times.

Though Washington spoke out against political parties, they soon emerged. Thomas Jefferson was the first liberal to be President, and his victory signaled the "Revolution of 1800." Another "common man" who took office was Andrew Jackson.

Until the twentieth century, most Presidents were weak. The only ones considered much stronger than Congress were Jackson, Abraham Lincoln, and Theodore Roosevelt. Woodrow Wilson had a bit more clout, but the Senate never ratified his Treaty of Versailles. However, since 1933, the Presidency has been a much more powerful office.

Although Andrew Jackson was famous for his veto that killed the Bank of the US, it should be restated that *vetoes are not the norm*. The greatest veto power was exhibited by Democrats Grover Cleveland and Franklin D. Roosevelt.

When one party controls the Legislative Branch, and another is in charge in the White House, more vetoes occur. As stated earlier, vetoes are rarely overridden. Andrew Johnson, the first President to be impeached, suffered the greatest percentage of overridden vetoes.

Definition: Presidential Approval Rating

This is a simple poll that's taken to survey if people believe the President is doing a good job.

Factors that make the approval rating go up: Good economy, new President, popular military event, and good use of the media.

Factors that make approval rating go down: Bad economy, unpopular war, and scandal. Presidents who serve two terms often experience a decreased approval rating in their second term.

Definition: Presidential Succession

If the President can't perform his or her duties, resigns, or dies in office, the Vice President takes over. Next in line would be the Speaker of the House, followed by the President pro tempore of the Senate. Then would come the cabinet leaders, starting with the Secretary of State, Treasury, and Defense.

Following the Secretary of Defense, it would go onward down the list of cabinet positions. When the President gives the State of the Union Address to the government, there's always one high-ranking official in an undisclosed location…just in case.

The *Twenty-Fifth Amendment* clarified the rules for replacing a President and filling a vacancy in the Vice Presidency. Today, if a President goes in for surgery, the Vice President can become *Acting President*. The *Presidential Succession Act of 1947* established the modern order of succession after the Vice President.

Definition: Lame Duck

A lame duck is a politician who has either lost a reelection bid, or their term in office is ending. For most elected officials, there are a few months between the election and the date they leave office. In that time period, there isn't much they can get done, as their political clout has been limited.

Though the term applies to all politicians, it's commonly used with Presidents. Assuming they are healthy, all Presidents (even if they win reelection) will be lame ducks, as the Presidency has **term-limits**. Congress and the Senate don't have term-limits, so incumbents can keep running for office for decades. Still, at some point, they will likely become lame ducks as well.

Review Questions

1. Which of the following is true about the Presidency?
   A) There are no term limits
   B) The President has the power to declare war
   C) The President can appoint Representatives and Senators
   D) The President can't veto a bill after five days
   E) The President can receive ambassadors

2. Why does a closed primary limit democracy of the average citizen?
   A) It is only open to those who are members of a particular political party
   B) Secret ballots are never used in a closed primary
   C) Only superdelegates can take part in a closed primary
   D) The Democratic Party is the only one that uses closed primaries
   E) Closed primaries have more superdelegates at stake than open primaries

3. All of the following are members of the Executive Office of the President (EOP) EXCEPT
   A) Office of Administration
   B) National Security Staff
   C) Office of Management and Budget
   D) Federal Reserve Board
   E) Council on Environmental Quality

4. An example of executive privilege would be a President who
   A) uses extensive military force without the consent of Congress
   B) consults the Senate for advice on a judicial appointee
   C) refuses to give classified executive information to Congress
   D) neglects to give Congress budgetary information
   E) wishes to assemble a special session of Congress

5. Which is true of independent regulatory agencies?
   A) They are a part of the Judicial Branch
   B) Many officials have job security and are difficult to remove
   C) Their creation can be found in the Bill of Rights
   D) The President can't appoint officials to any of them
   E) They can't issue mandates to the states

6. Who is the leader of the Department of Justice?
   A) Vice President
   B) Secretary of State
   C) Secretary of the Interior
   D) Chief of Staff
   E) Attorney General

7. Today, when would a President be a lame duck?
   A) Immediately after the first inauguration
   B) Just before the first term begins
   C) Just before the second term is completed
   D) Just before the third term begins
   E) After the third term ends

8. The War Powers Act was created primarily to
   A) limit the President's power to use military force abroad without the consent of Congress
   B) give the President more power in military operations
   C) permit the President to declare war instead of Congress
   D) eliminate executive privilege in foreign relations
   E) decrease the power of the President in terms of making treaties with foreign nations

9. In the Electoral College's winner-take-all scenario, a state's electoral votes go to the candidate with
   A) the most superdelegates
   B) a majority of the state's votes
   C) the most primary delegates
   D) the most votes in exit polling
   E) a plurality of all votes cast in the state

10. Who is next in line for the Presidency after the President and Vice President?
    A) Chief of Staff
    B) Secretary of Defense
    C) Speaker of the House
    D) Secretary of State
    E) President pro tempore of the Senate

Free-Response Questions

I. The President of the United States has many powers. However, unlike an absolute monarch, the power of the President can be limited.
   A. Identify three formal powers of the President that can be found in the Constitution. [p. 56]
   B. Describe two ways in which the President's power can be limited. [pp. 56, 59]
   C. Explain the role of executive privilege, and how it either decreases or increases the power of the President. [pp. 59-60]

II. George Washington assembled the first cabinet. A cabinet has become vital for a President, as enforcing the nation's laws has become a job not worthy of one person.
   A. Explain the function and importance of the following three positions. [p. 57]
      • Secretary of State
      • Secretary of Defense
      • Attorney General
   B. The Executive Office of the President is also vital in assisting the everyday operations of the White House. Explain the function and importance of both of the following. [p. 57]
      • Office of Management and Budget
      • National Security Council
   C. Independent regulatory agencies can be instrumental in enforcing laws. Identify one independent regulatory agency, and explain their specific role in government. [pp. 57-59]

Answers and Explanations

1. **E**. Receiving ambassadors is one of many formal powers of the Presidency. Other formal powers include making treaties, appointing officials, and acting as Commander-in-Chief of the military.

2. **A**. Unlike open primaries, closed primaries are only open to members who have pledged to be in a political party.

3. **D**. The Federal Reserve Board is independent, and not a part of the Executive Office of the President.

4. **C**. Conversations in the White House are kept confidential. To protect against publicizing classified information, the President and other high-ranking Executive Branch workers can refuse to give information to Congress or any court. This is called executive privilege.

5. **B**. Although the President appoints the board members of these agencies, they are difficult to remove from office.

6. **E**. The Attorney General is the leader of the Department of Justice, and makes sure that the rights of citizens are protected.

7. **C**. A lame duck is a President who is politically weak because they're about to leave office. They have either lost an election, or their term is up. Remember, there is a two-term limit to the Presidency because of the Twenty-Second Amendment. The lame duck period is from early November-January 20.

8. **A**. After the Vietnam War, the War Powers Act was passed, stating that the President can't use extensive overseas force (for more than 60 days followed by a 30-day withdrawal period) without the consent of Congress. In addition, Congress must be consulted at least 48 hours before the military is deployed.

9. **E**. Remember, it's not the majority (one more than half) in a Presidential Election…it's the ***plurality***, or the greatest amount of votes in the state. If there are more than two candidates who are popular, a majority of votes might be impossible.

10. **C**. If the President can't perform his or her duties, resigns, or dies in office, the Vice President takes over. Next would be the Speaker of the House, and the President pro tempore of the Senate. Following in line are the cabinet positions, starting with the Secretary of State, Treasury, and Defense.

The Judicial Branch

Somewhat cloaked in secrecy, the Judicial Branch wields immense power when interpreting laws and referencing them with the Constitution. By exhibiting their power of judicial review, they can determine if laws are constitutional or not. But how should a justice act? Being appointed for life, they are free from many political pressures. However, different justices act in various ways depending on the case they are hearing. The Supreme Court's important decisions have changed the way Americans live. Controversial issues such as abortion, civil rights, free speech, and rights of the accused, have all made their way through the court's chambers.

HERE'S WHAT YOU NEED TO KNOW:
Question: How is the Federal Court System organized?

Answer: See the chart below for specifics, but in simple terms:

Trials are held at one of the 94 US District Courts. They make decisions regarding issues such as federal crimes and federal civil suits. Those decisions can be appealed to the US Appellate Courts. The final appeal would go to the US Supreme Court.

The Federal Court System

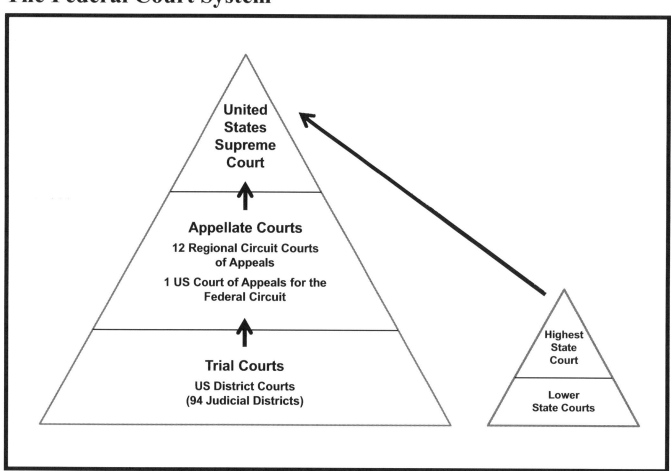

Question: How does the Supreme Court operate?

Answer: Article III of the Constitution created the Judicial Branch and the Supreme Court. Today, there are 9 justices (which include the Chief Justice) on the high court. After hearing a case, each justice votes. One justice will write the *majority opinion*, which is the winning decision. One of the justices on the losing side will write the *dissenting opinion*. Also to know:

1. They hear cases that involve Constitutional issues.

2. They can overturn cases that come out of the lower federal courts and the highest court of each state.

3. To get to the Supreme Court, there's an *appeals process (appellate jurisdiction)* where cases first must go through lower federal or state courts. A higher court can then hear the case. Much rarer is *original jurisdiction*, which means that cases involving ambassadors, foreign ministers, or state vs. state, can go *directly* to the Supreme Court.

4. Majority decisions of the court will overturn older cases, strike down laws, or affirm laws (keep them). The court can overturn a Legislative or Executive act in a process called *judicial review*. The first judicial review case was John Marshall's *Marbury* v. *Madison* (explained later).

Question: How might special interests affect who is appointed to the Supreme Court?

Answer: Because the President appoints justices for life, and there are only 9 of them, the selection is a big deal. Usually the appointee will have a similar ideology, or be of the same political party, as the President.

Special interest groups can affect which justice is appointed. Because potential justices have a record of how they voted on previous cases, their political ideology is not too much of a mystery. Therefore, a President (especially in the first term) can be susceptible to special interests who back those appointees who they believe will support their agenda. Interest groups hold political clout, and can help sway a President to appoint a justice.

If an appointee does not have experience, or has an ideology contrary to special interests, those interests can spend money on campaigns swaying public opinion against the appointment. In addition, because the Senate has to approve all appointees, Senators might also be influenced to approve or disapprove a justice.

Once approved to sit on the court, the justices can still be checked. Besides having their reputation at stake for unpopular decisions, justices could also be impeached for "high crimes and misdemeanors." Also, the size of the court could be increased by Congress, and new laws and amendments can be passed to circumvent (go around) their decisions.

Question: How has the Supreme Court become more inclusive of gender and race?

Answer: Over the last few decades, more women and minorities have been appointed to the court. Lyndon Johnson appointed Thurgood Marshall, the first African American justice, in 1967. Ronald Reagan delivered on a campaign promise and appointed the first female justice, Sandra Day O'Connor, in 1981. In 2009, Barack Obama appointed Sonia Sotomayor, the first Hispanic justice.

Definition: Judicial Review, John Marshall, and *Marbury* v. *Madison*, 1803

Supreme Court Chief Justice John Marshall increased the power of the federal government.

More importantly, he was known for judicial review.

In *Marbury* v. *Madison*, Marshall struck down a federal law for the first time ever. **The process whereby the Supreme Court determines if a law is constitutional is called judicial review.** Marshall's decision in the case declared the Judiciary Act of 1789 unconstitutional.

If you want more information: John Adams appointed Federalist "midnight judges" in the last days of his Presidency which were created by the Judiciary Act of 1801. He wanted to make these appointments before Thomas Jefferson and the Democratic-Republicans took office. Federalist William Marbury never received his job commission from the next Secretary of State, James Madison. He went to the Supreme Court to get a *writ of mandamus* (court order to force Madison to deliver his appointment). Although the Judiciary Act of 1789 said one could obtain a writ, the Constitution said nothing about going directly to the Supreme Court for such a matter. Hence, the law was unconstitutional.

You need to know other John Marshall decisions. All relevant court cases can be found together on the No Bull Review Sheet.

Definition: Writ of Certiorari

Lawyers from lower court decisions petition the Supreme Court to hear their case. When looking at these petitions, the Supreme Court can issue a **writ of certiorari**. A writ of certiorari is an order for that lower court to send up their records so the case can be heard. *It is granted when 4 of the 9 justices agree.* Only a very small percentage of requests for certiorari are accepted. The court generally will hear cases that have great public impact or need intense Constitutional interpretation.

Definition: Doctrine of Original Intent and Living Constitution

Until we can bring people back from the dead, we'll never know for sure what the framers had in mind. The doctrine of *original intent* is used to try to figure out what the Founding Fathers were thinking when they wrote the Constitution.

The opposite viewpoint would be the **"living Constitution."** Similar to loose interpretation (discussed in Chapter 1), a living document means that it can be interpreted generously and grow over time with each new generation.

For example, had the US lived with original intent, slavery would not have been abolished in 1865, as many of the framers were not abolitionists. In that regard, the Constitution was a living document. For some of today's issues, such as same-sex marriage and abortion, original intent would not be applicable, as the issues were not spoken about freely in 1787.

Question: What are other important tidbits to know about the Supreme Court?

Answer:

1. The Supreme Court generally chooses the cases that it wants to hear.

2. Only a small number of the cases appealed to the Supreme Court are actually heard.

3. Especially when a case is appealed from a state, it could take years for one to get to the Supreme Court. There are exceptions, as in the Presidential Election of 2000, the case of **Bush v. Gore** flew to the Supreme Court. The case involved George W. Bush's campaign's desire to end Al Gore's campaign's sponsoring of hand-counting ballots in the Florida Election.

The Court agreed with Bush, and the counting was stopped.

4. The Supreme Court is usually out of the public eye, and does fewer interviews than Congress or the President. They also don't look to interfere with arguments between the other two branches.

Definition: Judicial activism and judicial restraint

These terms are opposites. *Judicial activism* is the belief that the Supreme Court should rely on its personal views and be active in addressing social and political issues and policies. *Judicial restraint* means that the court should "restrain" itself from addressing such issues, and leave policy-making to the Legislative Branch.

Definition: *Stare decisis*

This means "let the decision stand." The courts often refer to other relevant cases when citing opinions. As seen in *common law*, decisions set a precedent. Therefore similar cases are decided in a similar fashion.

However, *stare decisis* can only go so far. The Supreme Court often overturns itself. As seen in *Plessy* v. *Ferguson* and *Brown* v. *Board of Education of Topeka*, Kansas (explained later), sometimes the social climate of the country and the mood of the court will change. Each new decision replaces the old one.

Question: How can the Supreme Court be checked?

Answer: The Legislative Branch can check the Judicial Branch by increasing the size of the Supreme Court, impeaching justices, confirming justices, and proposing amendments to the Constitution.

After key New Deal legislation was overturned in *Schechter Poultry Corp.* v. *US* (1935), and *US vs. Butler* (1936), Franklin D. Roosevelt had a plan to "pack the court." If Congress increases the size of the court, then the President can appoint justices with a similar ideology. His court packing plan was controversial, and he never went through with it. However, the plan was indeed constitutional.

Question: What types of trials are there in the judicial system?

Answer: The Bill of Rights guarantees the accused a public trial. *Litigation* is the act of bringing about legal proceedings. Facts of cases are explained in documents called *briefs*. Briefs are used for trials that are:

1. **Criminal** - cases that involve people who break the law. Note that in most criminal cases, there is no trial, as a **plea bargain** is reached. This means that the prosecutor and defense attorney have worked it out so that the defendant has pleaded guilty to fewer or less significant crimes.

2. **Civil** - Cases that resolve arguments between individuals. Lawsuits can only occur if there is reasonable **standing** to sue. In civil trials, the one who brings forth the lawsuit is called the *plaintiff*. The one being litigated against is the *defendant*.

Definition: Class-action suit

These are cases that are brought to court by an individual who is representing not only themselves, but also others who have suffered similar experiences. For example, the famous case of *Brown* v. *Board of Education of Topeka, Kansas* (explained later) was a class-action suit on behalf of African American schoolchildren.

Definition: *Amicus curiae*

In addition to the lawyers of both sides, outsiders can have a say in a case. ***Amicus curiae*** means "a friend of the court." *Amicus curiae* briefs come from a person who believes they have information that is useful for the court's evaluation of a case. *Amicus curiae* briefs are often used by special interest groups.

Review Questions

1. What is the significance of the Supreme Court's decision in *Marbury* v. *Madison*?
   A) The Supreme Court ruled that interstate commerce was controlled by the federal government
   B) Contracts must be honored at the state and federal levels
   C) The principle of judicial review was exercised to declare a law unconstitutional
   D) Slaves were not allowed to sue in court
   E) Factions would be controlled by a system of checks and balances

2. Which of the following Supreme Court techniques utilizes a previous case's decision?
   A) *Stare decisis*
   B) *Amicus curiae*
   C) Judicial activism
   D) Judicial restraint
   E) Writ of mandamus

3. Which of the following issues would be most relevant for today's "living Constitution"?
   A) Interstate commerce
   B) War declaration
   C) Powers of the President
   D) Quartering of troops
   E) Same-sex marriage

4. All of these statements about trials are true EXCEPT:
   A) Criminal trials involve people who broke the law
   B) Most cases do not end in plea bargains
   C) The plaintiff is the one who brings a suit to court
   D) Lawsuits can only occur if there is good standing
   E) Briefs explain the facts of a case

5. All of the following are checks on the judicial system EXCEPT:
   A) Impeachment of judges
   B) Congress can increase the size of the Supreme Court
   C) Presidential pardons
   D) Amendments can be proposed
   E) Congress can overturn court decisions with a 2/3 vote

6. What would a writ of certiorari be used for?
   A) Appointing a justice to the Supreme Court
   B) Allowing documents to be provided by a "friend of the court"
   C) Plea bargaining in a criminal trial
   D) Sending up documents from a lower court
   E) Establishing a class-action suit

7. Most of the cases that reach the Supreme Court involve
   A) ambassadors
   B) foreign nations
   C) state vs. state arguments
   D) appellate jurisdiction
   E) writs of mandamus

8. The idea that the judicial branch shouldn't preoccupy itself with making policy is called
   A) judicial review
   B) judicial activism
   C) *amicus curiae*
   D) *stare decisis*
   E) judicial restraint

9. John Marshall's longest lasting legacy involves
   A) strengthening the power of the Supreme Court
   B) increasing the number of justices that sit on the Supreme Court
   C) upholding the Judiciary Act of 1789
   D) giving states the right to nullify laws seen as unjust
   E) establishing the doctrine of original intent

10. Which of the following is the most binding?
    A) Amendment to US Constitution
    B) Supreme Court decision
    C) Executive Order
    D) Legislative statute
    E) State constitution

Free-Response Questions

I. The goal of the Judicial Branch is to interpret laws and make sure that the Constitution is being obeyed. Although the Supreme Court is the highest court in the land, there are other courts which decide cases way before they ever get to the top.
  A. Distinguish between original and appellate jurisdiction. [p. 67]
  B. Describe two of the following, and indicate their importance in the legal system.
- *Amicus Curiae* [p. 70]
- Class Action Suit [p. 69]
- Plea Bargain [p. 69]

  C. Define writ of certiorari. Explain its importance in the process of how a case can get to the Supreme Court. [p. 68]

II. The life of the Supreme Court justice can be a mystery to the outsider. Because they rarely do media interviews, it's hard to get into the head of the nine people who sit on the high court.
  A. Explain the process of how a justice is appointed. [p. 67]
  B. Indicate one way in which special interests can affect the appointment process. [p. 67]
  C. Distinguish between judicial activism and judicial restraint. [p. 69]
  D. Distinguish between *original intent* and a *living Constitution* [p. 68]

Answers and Explanations

1. **C.** John Marshall's court used judicial review. The court can interpret if laws are constitutional or not. The law in question in this case was the Judiciary Act of 1789.

2. **A.** *Stare decisis* means "let the decision stand." The courts often refer to other relevant cases when citing opinions. As seen in *common law*, decisions set a precedent. Therefore similar cases are decided in likewise fashion.

3. **E.** Similar to loose interpretation, a living document means that the Constitution can be interpreted generously and grow over time with each new generation. Original intent (the intent of the framers) is not feasible for same-sex marriage.

4. **B.** Criminal cases are usually plea bargained, and a trial doesn't occur. This means the prosecutor and defense attorney have worked it out so that the defendant has pleaded guilty to fewer or less significant crimes.

5. **E.** Although Congress can reword legislation to go around a court's decision, they can't overturn the Supreme Court's decision.

6. **D.** A writ of certiorari is an order to send up documents so a case can be heard at the Supreme Court.

7. **D.** Most of the cases that reach the Supreme Court involve appeals from lower courts, such as the highest court of each state. Original jurisdiction occurs far less than appellate jurisdiction.

8. **E.** Judicial activism is the belief that the Supreme Court should be active in addressing social and political issues and policies. Judicial restraint means that the court should "restrain" itself from addressing such issues, and leave policy-making to the Legislative Branch.

9. **A.** John Marshall helped make the Supreme Court the powerful entity it is today. He strengthened both the power of the court, and the might of the federal government.

10. **A.** An Amendment is just as binding as anything else in the Constitution…and the Constitution is the highest law of the land!

Executive Branch Bureaucracy and Public Policy

Congress and the President can't do all of the work by themselves. Millions of government workers are needed to regulate and control the daily activities of the government. At state and national levels we call these workers *bureaucrats*. Though they are controlled by law, they can use their discretion to make important decisions.

Their decisions help to establish *public policy*, or the actions taken by the government to solve problems and react to issues. Along with Congress, which legislates public policy, the bureaucracy helps the Executive Branch enforce it. Public policy comes in many forms such as social welfare, military, energy, environment, and health. Also important are monetary and fiscal policies, as the nation's economy depends on actions by the Federal Reserve as well as the budgetary powers of the President and Congress.

HERE IS WHAT YOU NEED TO KNOW:
• EXECUTIVE BRANCH BUREAUCRACY
Definition: Bureaucracy

Bureaucrats are civil servants, or those who work for the government on behalf of the people. The *bureaucracy* is the enormous and specified hierarchy of government jobs that run both states and the nation. Today, there are millions of bureaucratic workers at all levels of government. They have expertise in their field, and are hard to remove from office.

Because they are so large, bureaucracies have been criticized for *duplication*, or when different offices do the same tasks. Critics call this a waste of resources. Also, *red tape* becomes a problem, as rules seen as ridiculous by the public have to be followed to get something done.

Question: How does one become a bureaucrat?

Answer: Today, jobs are based on the **merit system**, where intelligence, competency, and experience can lead to employment. In the nineteenth-century however, the **patronage system** was popular. This was where campaign supporters received government jobs despite oftentimes being unqualified. Under Andrew Jackson, it was known as the spoils system. However, after the 1883 **Pendleton Act** was passed, a **civil service test** was established to confirm the competency of an applicant.

Question: What types of jobs make up the federal bureaucracy?

Answer: Most important to know are those discussed in the Executive Branch chapter, such as:
1. Cabinet
2. Independent Executive Agencies
3. Independent Regulatory Agencies
4. Government Corporations - Businesses run by the national government, such as the Federal Deposit Insurance *Corporation*, which insures bank deposits, and the Postal Service. So yes, your letter-carrier is part of the bureaucracy.

Question: Since the early twentieth century, what has happened to the size of the bureaucracy?

Answer: It has ballooned...BIG TIME. Two large escalations occurred in the twentieth century. First, during the Progressive Era c1900-1920, new agencies, such as the ***Food and***

Drug Administration, were created to look after the health and well-being of consumers and citizens. All of these new agencies needed workers. So, thousands were hired and became bureaucrats. In the 1930s, Franklin D. Roosevelt's New Deal created dozens of new offices to help cope with the Great Depression. All of those agencies also needed workers. The size of government increased, as specialization of jobs became common.

Question: How can the federal bureaucracy be checked?
Answer:
The President can make appointments to certain offices, which are subject to approval by the Senate.

The Legislative Branch has a great say in the budget, and controls how much funding goes into bureaucratic agencies. They can also conduct investigations and pass laws which affect bureaucrats.

The Supreme Court can declare acts of Congress, which might favor the bureaucracy, unconstitutional. Outside of the Supreme Court, lawsuits can be brought against the bureaucracy.

Definition: Bureaucratic Discretion
It would be impossible for Congress and the President to control the everyday operations of the bureaucracy. Often, policy is not written down in law. Therefore, it is up to bureaucrats to make decisions based on their discretion. After all, a bureaucrat is more of an expert in their field than a Congressional committee.

Therefore, the Federal Trade Commission would be the one to determine unfair business practices. The Federal Communications Commission would indicate grounds for establishing a non-commercial educational radio station. They could also penalize a radio "shock jock."

Definition: Casework
Representatives do ***casework*** to help constituents deal with problems and navigate through the bureaucracy. They, or their staff of caseworkers, can answer questions and point people in the right direction. Though they can't get an agency to rule a certain way, they can cut through some red tape and help citizens deal with the large and confusing bureaucracy. For example, a Representative can help a constituent contact the Social Security Administration if they are having a problem obtaining benefits. Of course, dealing with such business can be tedious, and could drain on a representative's time. However, keeping constituents happy can ensure reelection.

• **PUBLIC POLICY**
Definition: Monetary and Fiscal Policy
Let's distinguish between these two economic policies. In the Executive Branch chapter, we learned that the Federal Reserve Board (the Fed) controls how money is circulated. They are involved in ***monetary policy***, which means controlling the supply and circulation of money, and how much it costs to borrow it.

If the Federal Reserve Board believes that too much money is in circulation (thereby causing inflation), they can make money more expensive to borrow by ***raising interest rates*** on loans. The higher the interest rate, the more debt one has to pay off in their loan.

If the economy takes a downturn, as it did in 2009, they can ***cut interest rates*** to make money readily available. When they cut interest rates, mortgages and car loans become very cheap, and people start to spend more. The Fed gives money to banks at what's called the *discount rate*. The banks then loan the money to the public at a higher rate to make a profit.

Another measure used to control inflation is buying and selling government bonds and securities. When the Fed buys bonds, money supply increases and the economy expands. When the Fed sells bonds, money supply decreases and the economy contracts.

The Fed can also increase and decrease the *reserve requirement* for its member banks. This is the set amount of money that banks must hold on to. If the Fed increases this requirement, then banks have less money to lend out. If they decrease it, then banks can help the economy expand by lending out more money.

Fiscal policy relates to government spending and taxation. For fiscal policy, we need to understand the budget (explained next).

Question: How is the federal budget created?

Answer: In a *fiscal year*, the budget goes from October 1 until September 30 of the following year. Thousands of people within both the Legislative and Executive Branches work to pass *appropriation bills* for spending. About 2/3 of the budget is filled with **uncontrollable, or mandatory spending**. This refers to budget expenditures that can't be eliminated by law. Many of these are entitlement programs such as welfare and Social Security. The part of the budget that can be changed is called *discretionary spending*. You should know:

1. The President proposes the budget. Much of the work is done by the *Office of Management and Budget* and *Council of Economic Advisors*, both within the EOP (Executive Office of the President). To spend more on programs, **either more money has to be raised through taxes, or cuts to other programs are necessary**.

2. If cuts need to be made, the respective agencies are asked where the cuts should come from. In other words, if the Department of Agriculture is losing money, they know better than the President as where to cut.

3. The independent staff agency, the *Congressional Budget Office* helps Congress analyze the budget. Notice how both the President and Congress have budget agencies looking over their shoulders.

4. The House and Senate Budget Committees come up with *budget resolutions*, which establish the maximum amount of money they feel should be spent in different areas. Next, a *reconciled* bill from both Houses is voted on. Finally, the *appropriation (spending) bills* are passed to reserve the money needed for all of the budget expenditures.

5. The President then signs the appropriation bills. Of course, by that time the House and Senate could have put items into the budget that the President doesn't like. Usually, the President will have to tolerate unwanted material.

The President must spend what is allocated, as *impoundment of funds* (not spending) is prevented by the *Budget and Impoundment Control Act of 1974*. Funds must be spent unless Congress approves otherwise.

NOTE: From year to year the budget is very similar. However, just a small percentage in cuts will have a large negative impact on programs and agencies.

Definition: Keynesian Economics vs. Supply Side Theory

You should know these two economic theories:

Keynesian economics involves deficit spending...to spend more money than you have. It was the theory of British economist John Maynard Keynes, and was used by Franklin D. Roosevelt during the Great Depression. Roosevelt wanted to spend, spend, spend...so he could fix, fix, fix. This stimulation of the economy is called *pump priming*. The hope is to create jobs, so more people have money to put into the economy. To increase revenue, the government can sell bonds and raise taxes.

In his economic policy of *Reaganomics*, Ronald Reagan supported wealthy businesses so that profits would "trickle down" to all classes. This was related to *supply-side economics* theory where less government regulation and tax breaks would lead to more investment and job creation. Reagan also cut certain programs to decrease the government's workforce.

Definition: Balanced Budget Act of 1985/ Budget Control Act of 2011

When the government spends more money than it has, it ends up with a deficit. The *national debt* is the measure of how much money the government has borrowed to keep up with spending.

Also called the Gramm-Rudman-Hollings Act, the *Balanced Budget and Emergency Deficit Control Act of 1985* looked to get rid of the national deficit and bring about a balanced budget. To do this, the bill called for a *sequester*, or across-the-board cuts by percentage to all federal programs.

In 2011, President Obama signed the *Budget Control Act*. This act raised the *debt ceiling*, which is the national debt limit and legal amount of money the United States can borrow (favored by Democrats). It also promised to cut spending and gradually reduce the federal deficit (favored by Republicans). The Act also threatened a sequester for 2013.

Question: How are taxes collected?

Part of the Treasury Department, the *Internal Revenue Service* (IRS) is in charge of enforcing tax laws and collecting taxes. Our system of income tax is called a *graduated or progressive income tax*, where the more someone makes, the higher their tax rate. This was a product of the *Sixteenth Amendment*.

Question: What should I know about Environmental and Energy Policy?

The *Environmental Protection Agency* (EPA) of the Executive Branch enforces environmental regulations on everything from air pollution to water contamination. You should know the *Clean Air Act of 1970*, which looked to reduce air pollution and auto emissions, and The Water Pollution Control Act of 1972, which aimed to rid rivers and lakes of pollution. Also stated earlier, many environmental laws are *unfunded mandates*, where the states must pay their way into compliance.

The environmental policies tie into energy. Today, there's a huge demand for energy, but the way we get it can hurt the environment. *Drilling for oil* has been one way to get more energy, but sometimes it leads to highly-publicized oil spills. A new method, called *fracking*, looks to fracture rocks to get natural gas. This too has led to fears of environmental contamination. *Nuclear power* has been an alternative for years, but it has destructive potential. Although the United States is looking to decrease their dependence on foreign oil, energy and environmental advocates continue to arm-twist to find a compromise.

Question: What should I know about health care policy?

Health care has been, and still is, a highly debated topic. In the United States, coverage has historically been a private matter with people purchasing health plans themselves, or through employers. Publicly, you need to know about Medicare and Medicaid. They were part of Lyndon Johnson's **Great Society**, which was a plan to help the poor, minorities, and the disadvantaged.

Medicare became a part of Social Security in 1965, offering senior citizens health insurance.

Medicaid is also a 1965 program that was created to help people with low income cope with medical expenses.

Passed in 2010, the **Patient Protection and Affordable Care Act**, also known as the **Affordable Care Act**, is commonly known as President Barack Obama's *Obamacare*. The act looks to lower health care costs and make health insurance more affordable. The law was upheld by the Supreme Court in 2012 in *National Federation of Independent Business* v. *Sebelius*.

Question: What should I know about military policy?

Throughout this review book, we have discussed much about foreign policy and military policy. Here's a brief history of US military policy. You should know:

1. George Washington wanted the United States to stay neutral and free from alliances.

2. The United States had been neutral for much of its history up to World War I and World War II.

3. After World War II, **the role of the President expanded, as the policy of containment** (stopping the spread of communism during the Cold War) led the US into several military conflicts, including Korea and Vietnam. With the ***Gulf of Tonkin Resolution***, Congress gave President Lyndon Johnson a "blank check" to escalate forces. Military spending ballooned during the Cold War, especially in the 1980s with programs such as Ronald Reagan's Strategic Defense Initiative (better known as Star Wars).

4. After communism fell in the Soviet Union and Eastern Europe, many defense measures were cut. Defense spending increased greatly after the US was attacked on 9/11/2001, as the military was deployed to Afghanistan and Iraq.

Definition: Iron Triangle

Committee ... Interest Group ... Agency. These are the three components of the *iron triangle*. All three work together to make public policy. Their relationship is so solid, it's considered to be iron. Here's how it works:

Interest groups lobby Congress with campaign finance and other incentives ➡ Congressional Committees propose legislation for the programs that the interest groups favor, and they fund the agencies who regulate those programs ➡ Agencies, or bureaucrats who regulate industry, are also pressured by the special interests. They just might regulate the way those interests, and Congress, want.

Let's use a simple example for this complex entity. Let's say *No Bull Review Books* is a special interest. No Bull gives lots of money to Congressional officers who use it to campaign and stay in power. Let's say there's a Review Book Agency that determines how a book should look. Congress funds that agency, who it just so happens, regulates *just* the way No Bull likes it. Everyone's happy. No Bull wins, Congress has the electoral support they need, and the Review Book Agency just got a nice hefty budget for next year. It's iron-clad.

The Iron Triangle

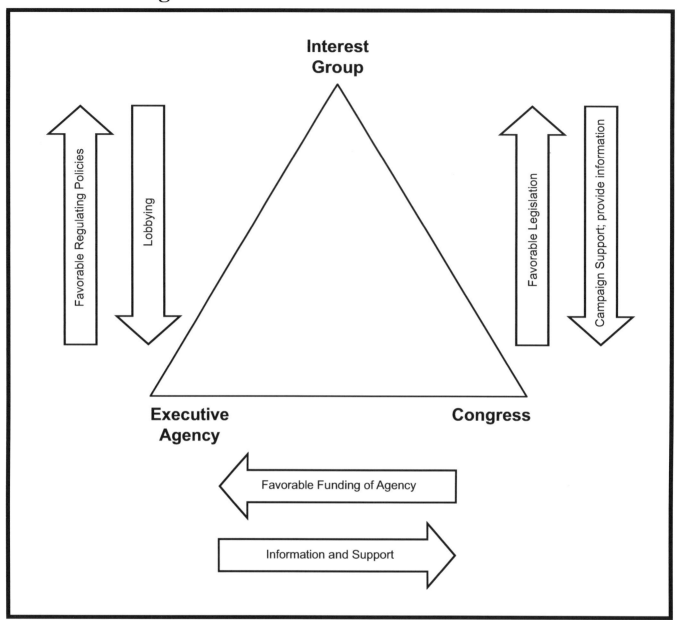

Definition: Issue Networks

This is a network of people looking for the same public policy changes. An issue network can include special interests, intellectuals, congressional staffs, journalists, and researchers of various fields. Remember: ***It's the issue that brings the network together***.

Let's say we wanted to stop texting while driving in National Parks. That would be supported by parent groups who want safe roads, cellphone carriers who don't want their product to cause harm, auto insurance companies who want lower rates, and the National Park Service who wants safer tourism. Ultimately, bureaucrats will hear their outcry and regulate accordingly.

Review Questions

1. Which of the following statements is true about the federal bureaucracy?
   A) It is biggest in the Judicial Branch
   B) It contains fewer jobs today than it did in 1933
   C) Congress does not legislate for all of their decisions
   D) All jobs must be confirmed by the Senate
   E) Bureaucrats can only be found at the national level

2. Which of the following is NOT in the federal bureaucracy?
   A) Post Office
   B) Independent Regulatory Agencies
   C) Federal Deposit Insurance Corporation
   D) Cabinet
   E) President pro tempore

3. Which is NOT considered in the bureaucratic hiring process?
   A) Problem-solving abilities
   B) Experience in one's field
   C) How competent one appears
   D) Political support for candidates
   E) How trustworthy an applicant is

4. Which of the following types of policies is the Federal Reserve concerned with?
   A) Monetary
   B) Fiscal
   C) Environmental
   D) Military
   E) Energy

5. How has the Sixteenth Amendment affected fiscal policy?
   A) It provided the power for the Federal Reserve to cut interest rates
   B) It allows the President to start the budget process
   C) Higher tax rates are applied to those with higher income
   D) The President is not allowed to impound funds
   E) Money for entitlements can't be cut in a budget

6. Which is the best example of Keynesian Economics?
   A) Ronald Reagan's tax cuts
   B) Budget Control Act
   C) Franklin D. Roosevelt's New Deal
   D) Harry Truman's policy of containment
   E) Lyndon Johnson's Gulf of Tonkin Resolution

7. Who of the following would be LEAST involved in the federal budget process?
   A) Congressional Budget Office
   B) Department of the Interior
   C) Office of Management and Budget
   D) President pro tempore
   E) House of Representatives

8. Which of the following is an example of mandatory spending in a budget?
   A) Social Security
   B) Military spending
   C) Renewable energy investments
   D) Space Exploration investments
   E) National Parks spending

9. Congress can check the President's military power in all of the following ways EXCEPT:
A) Refusing to approve an appointment
B) Budgeting less money to the military
C) Not ratifying a treaty
D) Utilizing the War Powers Resolution
E) Declaring Executive Orders null and void

10. What has been a major criticism of iron triangles?
A) Policy can be manipulated to benefit special interests
B) Too much power is centered in the Executive Branch
C) They only favor one political party
D) It gives too many jobs out to liberals through the revolving door
E) They destroy the integrity of issue networks

Free-Response Questions

I. The bureaucracy has become a powerful arm of the Executive Branch. Since the early 1900s, the size of the bureaucracy has ballooned in size, generating immense impact at both federal and state levels.

   A. Explain how the bureaucracy is configured. [p. 75]

   B. Identify two ways in which the bureaucracy can be checked by the Legislative and/or Executive Branch. [p. 76]

   C. Describe how one of the following can affect the decisions of bureaucratic agencies.
- Issue networks [p. 80]
- Iron Triangles [pp. 79-80]

II. Governments establish public policy to solve problems and react to issues. Economic policy has become a complex process in the United States, with many eyes looking over legislation and decisions.

   A. Explain the difference between monetary and fiscal policy. [pp. 76-77]

   B. Identify two ways in which the Federal Reserve Board can affect the economy. [pp. 76-77]

   C. Describe the role of two of the following in the budget process. [pp. 77-78]
- President
- Congress
- Agencies

Answers and Explanations

1. **C**. Bureaucrats are permitted to use their discretion on many decisions. They are more specialized and knowledgeable in their field than most members of Congress.

2. **E**. The President pro tempore leads the Senate. Congress is not a member of the bureaucracy. They are elected officials who can control the bureaucracy.

3. **D**. The merit system looked to get rid of patronage, or hiring those based on their political ties. The merit system looks to award jobs to those who deserve it.

4. **A**. The Fed is concerned with monetary policy and how the US Dollar is circulated. Fiscal policy involves creation of the federal budget, taxing, and spending.

5. **C**. The Sixteenth Amendment provided for a graduated or progressive income tax, where the more you make, the higher the tax rate.

6. **C**. Franklin D. Roosevelt's New Deal looked to spend more money than the government had. Deficit spending looks to pump more money into the economy so jobs can be created.

7. **B**. The Department of the Interior protects natural resources, including National Parks, and honors culture and Native American tribal communities.

8. **A**. Social Security and Medicare are entitlements that can't legally be removed from a budget.

9. **E**. Congress can check the military might of the President in several ways. However, it's up to the courts to determine if an Executive Order is unconstitutional.

10. **A**. In an iron triangle, special interests can influence Congress and the agencies that regulate.

Civil Liberty and Civil Rights

The Constitution and Bill of Rights define the freedoms that Americans live by. But to what extent are rights protected? Is freedom of speech absolute? Can every aspect of religion be protected? The Supreme Court has interpreted these freedoms for more than two centuries. Sometimes they have ruled against their earlier decisions when interpreting.

Although the courts have expanded protections of liberty that were long overdue, some decisions have come with criticism. Still, much of their actions have expanded civil rights (protections of equality and political rights) for African Americans and other minorities whose liberty, equality, and Constitutional protections had long been ignored.

HERE IS WHAT YOU NEED TO KNOW:
• **CIVIL LIBERTY**

Question: For this topic, what are the most important Amendments to know?

Answer: Here are the relevant ones for this topic:

Important Bill of Rights Amendments

1st - Freedoms of speech, press, religion, assembly, and right to petition the government.

2nd - Right to bear arms.

4th - Freedom from unreasonable searches and seizures.

5th - Due process rights (right to fair justice, and freedoms from self-incrimination). Also, one cannot be tried twice for the same crime. This is a freedom from "double-jeopardy."

6th - Right to a fair trial and attorney.

Other Amendments Relevant to this Chapter:

14th - Equality of citizenship, a due process clause for the states, and equal protection under the law, 1868.

15th - Universal male suffrage (voting), 1870.

24th - Ended the practice of poll taxes, 1964.

Question: To what extent is free speech in the First Amendment limited?

Answer: Free speech has several limitations. Here are two landmark cases that elaborate on free speech:

1. ***Schenck v. US, 1919*** - Charles Schenck was a member of the Socialist Party. He distributed thousands of leaflets containing damaging language against the World War I draft. Consequently, he was arrested for violating the Espionage Act, which made it illegal to disrupt the war effort. Weren't those leaflets protected by the free speech clause of the First Amendment?

The Supreme Court said "no." Free speech was not absolute, as Schenck was creating a ***"clear and present danger."*** According to Justice Oliver Wendell Holmes, Jr., Schenck's actions were like "shouting fire in a theater." Similarly, vocal anarchy was not tolerated in the states either, as decided in ***Gitlow v. NY*** (1925).

2. In the 1951 case of ***Dennis v. US***, the Supreme Court ruled that speech advocating for an overthrow of the government was not protected by the First Amendment. Eugene Dennis of the American Communist Party had violated the Smith Act of 1940, which made such talk a crime.

However, unlike the preceding two cases, the ***Texas v. Johnson*** (1989) decision expanded free speech. The Supreme Court ruled that burning of the American flag was protected by the First Amendment.

Definition: Establishment Clause and Free Exercise Clause

The First Amendment contains an ***establishment clause*** which states that Congress can't make a law establishing a religion. The amendment goes on to say that government can't interfere with the free exercise of religion. This is called the ***free exercise clause***.

Question: How has the Supreme Court interpreted the establishment and free exercise clauses?

The framers believed that the First Amendment built a ***"wall of separation"*** between Church and State. However, court cases have challenged this wall. You need to know:

1. ***Everson* v. *Board of Education, 1947*** - A New Jersey law permitted the busing of students to parochial schools (schools run by a religious organization). Since taxpayer money would be used for the buses, it seemed that the state was supporting a religion. The Supreme Court decided that the busing was constitutional, as benefitting students was the main purpose of the law, and not the support of a religious institution.

2. ***Engel* v. *Vitale, 1962*** - The Supreme Court ruled that official ***school-sponsored prayer*** is a violation of the free exercise clause of the First Amendment. Even if the prayer was non-denominational and optional, it was still unconstitutional.

3. ***Lemon* v. *Kurtzman, 1971*** - In Pennsylvania, non-public schools (many of which were Catholic) received public money for teachers who taught secular (non-religious) material. The Supreme Court ruled that this violated the Establishment Clause. Their decision created the ***"Lemon Test"*** where a government's laws:

    a. Had to be secular in its legislative purpose.

    b. Couldn't have the primary effect of advancing or inhibiting religion.

    c. Couldn't have an "excessive entanglement with religion."

4. ***Reynolds* v. *US, 1879*** —George Reynolds was a Mormon in Utah who had two wives. Although his religion allowed polygamy, it was against state law. He appealed his conviction to the Supreme Court, but the Court ruled that religion could not be used as a defense against polygamy, as the free exercise clause is not absolute.

5. ***Oregon* v. *Smith, 1990*** —The Supreme Court ruled that illegal drug use performed as part of a religious ceremony is still illegal drug use. The Employment Division of Oregon could therefore deny unemployment benefits to someone fired for such use of drugs.

Question: What do I need to know about the Fourteenth Amendment (1868)?

Answer: ***Reconstruction*** was a time period after the Civil War where former slaves were given rights. The Thirteenth Amendment abolished slavery. For the Fourteenth Amendment, you need to know:

1. The *citizenship clause*, stated that all persons native born or naturalized are citizens of both the US and their state.

2. The *due process clause* prevents *states* from depriving of life, liberty, or property without due process of law (The Fifth Amendment prevented the *federal government* from depriving life, liberty, or property without due process of law).

3. The *equal protection clause* makes sure that laws are applied to everyone equally.

You also need to understand what ***selective incorporation*** means. The Supreme Court has used the Fourteenth Amendment to apply certain federal protections of the Bill of Rights to the states. They have *selectively* applied these protections **one clause at a time in a piecemeal fashion**. Clauses within the Bill of Rights were selectively incorporated by the Warren Court (explained next).

Question: What cases of the Warren Court (1953-1969) are important to know?

Answer: Besides being a major factor in desegregation (explained later), *Earl Warren's Court* gave more rights to the accused. You should know:

1. ***Miranda* v. *Arizona, 1966*** - Ernesto Miranda admitted to charges of rape and kidnapping after a lengthy interrogation. Because he did not know that he had a right to remain silent, the Supreme Court ruled that Miranda did not receive fair due process. Since his Fifth Amendment rights were violated, he had to be retried. The controversy of the Warren Court's decision has changed the way police apprehend criminals. Today, a priority is the reading of "Miranda rights" upon arrest. Miranda was later retried and convicted. NOTE: The Fourteenth Amendment was also used to apply due process rights to the states.

2. ***Gideon* v. *Wainwright, 1963*** - Clarence Gideon was accused of breaking into a billiards establishment in Florida. At his trial, he was denied the right to an attorney because Florida would only appoint lawyers for capital (murder) offenses. He was found guilty. The Warren Court later ruled that Gideon's rights were violated. His Sixth Amendment rights to a fair trial should have applied to the state of Florida because of the Fourteenth Amendment's due process clause. He was retried and acquitted (found not guilty). Another case, *Escobedo* v. *Illinois*, involved a similar denial of the right to consult with an attorney.

3. ***Mapp* v. *Ohio, 1961*** - Dollree Mapp's house was searched in Ohio, as the police were looking for a fugitive. Instead, they found indecent pornographic material that violated the law. The police seized the evidence and Mapp was convicted. The Supreme Court heard Mapp's appeal, and ruled that the evidence was not admissible in court. This was because the protections of the Fourth Amendment (unreasonable searches and seizures) applied to the states through the Fourteenth Amendment's due process clause. You need to know that the ***exclusionary rule*** prohibits any evidence that was collected unconstitutionally to be admitted at a trial.

Definition: Freedom of Information Act (FOIA)

Passed in 1966, this act gave every citizen the right to access most federal agency records. Some files, however, are protected from full disclosure. Still, the act expands democracy by exposing many government records previously left classified.

A few decades later, the *Whistleblower Protection Act* was passed in 1989. This law protected agency workers who reported the misconduct of their peers.

Definition: Fair Labor Standards Act (FLSA)

The Fair Labor Standards Act of 1938 protected workers' rights by setting maximum working hours before overtime pay kicks in, and establishing a minimum wage law.

Definition: Brady Bill

The Brady Handgun Violence Prevention Act was named for former Press Secretary James

Brady, who was shot in an assassination attempt on President Reagan. The ***Brady Bill*** was passed in 1993, and expanded background checks to obtain firearms.

Definition: Patriot Act

After the terrorist attacks of 9/11/2001, the government wanted greater ability to detain and investigate suspected terrorists. The Patriot Act expanded the powers of law enforcement with regards to surveillance and investigation. The Act also permitted the detaining and deporting of suspected immigrant terrorists. Critics of the act say it violates civil liberties. Supporters believe it is necessary for America's safety.

• CIVIL RIGHTS
Definition: *Dred Scott* v. *Sandford*, 1857

Dred Scott was a slave who was taken to live in free northern territory. Because he lived on free soil for an extended period of time, he believed he had legal recourse to sue for his freedom. Chief Justice Roger B. Taney, on behalf of the Supreme Court, stated that:

1. Scott was a slave, which meant that he was not protected by the United States Constitution, and couldn't even sue in court.

2. Slave compromises (specifically the Missouri Compromise) which excluded slavery in certain states, were unconstitutional, as according to the Fifth Amendment, people could not be deprived of their property. Slaves were property.

The ruling of the Dred Scott case wouldn't be overturned until the Fourteenth Amendment was ratified in 1868.

Definition: Slaughterhouse Cases, 1873

These were cases that put into question the protections of the Fourteenth Amendment. Louisiana created a corporation for the slaughtering of livestock. This corporation put all of the local slaughterhouses out of work. The butchers who lost their jobs believed that the Louisiana creation was a violation of their Fourteenth Amendment right to exercise free trade equally. The butchers lost, as the Supreme Court stated that the Amendment did not protect "privileges and immunities of citizenship" ***in a state***. Therefore states could create a slaughterhouse for the health and safety of the public.

Definition: *Plessy* v. *Ferguson*, *1896* and Jim Crow

To understand segregation, let's go back to this 1896 case. Homer Plessy was part African American, but sat in a "white's only" railroad car. He was challenging the Separate Car Act of Louisiana which segregated blacks from whites on trains. The Supreme Court decided that "separate but equal" was Constitutional, even though the Fourteenth Amendment said that everyone was equal. ***"Separate but equal"*** meant that African Americans and whites could be segregated (separated), so long as their facilities were the same (which they typically weren't). Thus, ***Jim Crow laws*** were enforced in the South, as separate bathrooms, schools, drinking fountains, and restaurants existed until the 1960s.

Question: After Reconstruction, how did Southern states prevent African Americans from voting?

Answer: Despite the ***Fifteenth Amendment*** giving universal suffrage to men in 1870, Southern states had control over election voting and registration because both were reserved (state) powers. Southern states tried to ***disenfranchise*** (deny the right to vote) African Americans through:

1. Violence at the polls. Southern whites typically voted Democratic. Surely, African Americans would vote Republican, the party of Lincoln. There were no secret ballots back then, and intimidation played a part at the polls. As early as 1875, the *Mississippi Plan* organized such violence against African American voters.

2. A *poll tax*, or a tax to vote. Before voting, free blacks would have to present a receipt proving they paid their tax. The *Twenty-Fourth Amendment* would outlaw this practice in 1964.

3. *Literacy tests*. In order to vote, one had to pass a difficult exam. Whites would not have to take it because of the...

4. *Grandfather clause*. If your grandfather could vote in the Election of 1860, the literacy test would not disqualify you from voting. Newly-freed blacks' grandfathers had been slaves who couldn't vote.

Question: How did African Americans overcome discrimination?

Answer: During the *Civil Rights Era* of the 1950s and 1960s, things began to change. African American civil rights leaders such as Rosa Parks and Martin Luther King, Jr. practiced passive resistance (nonviolence), and civil disobedience to obtain political equality. *Civil disobedience* means not obeying laws that are seen as unjust. *Sit-ins* were great examples of civil disobedience, as African Americans challenged segregation laws by illegally sitting inside of "whites-only" restaurants. Through boycotts, marches, and speeches by those such as Martin Luther King, Jr., the climate began to change.

Definition: *Brown* v. *Board of Education of Topeka, Kansas, 1954*

In a landmark case (or really, five cases in one) for ending segregation in schools, a 9-0 decision of the *Warren Court* (named for Chief Justice Earl Warren) declared that "separate but equal" was inherently unequal. Thurgood Marshall, later a Supreme Court justice, argued on behalf of Linda Brown and a score of other black children who were denied integration. The NAACP was instrumental in constructing this case.

It should be noted that, although segregation under the law (called *de jure segregation*) was struck down, many communities still voluntarily segregate themselves today. This residential type of segregation is called *de facto segregation*.

Definition: Little Rock 9

After the *Brown* decision, controversy rocked Central High School in Little Rock, Arkansas. The nation's media focused on the violence here when nine students attempting to go to school were met by mobs of protesters. Governor Orval Faubus called in the Arkansas Guard to support segregation. However, President Eisenhower had the final say as Commander-in-Chief of the military and executer of laws. Ultimately, federal troops enforced integration.

Definition: Civil Rights Act of 1964 and Voting Rights Act of 1965

Signed by President Johnson after a lengthy filibuster (delay in vote), this act ended all major forms of discrimination and segregation. The *Equal Employment Opportunity Commission* (EEOC) was formed to enforce laws prohibiting discrimination in the workplace. NOTE: The Civil Rights Act of 1991 created more jury trials, and caps on damages regarding statutes enforced by the EEOC.

Still, civil rights were not absolute in Alabama. In 1965, students and civil rights activists marched from Selma to Montgomery demanding African American voter registration rights. Along the way, they were met with tear gas and violence from Alabama State Troopers.

Eventually, the **Voting Rights Act of 1965** was passed. This reiterated the wording of the Fifteenth Amendment and prevented discrimination when voting. Thus, the literacy test would be illegal. The law permitted the federal government to register voters in precincts where discrimination looked to be occurring. Part of this legislation was struck down in 2013, as the Supreme Court ruled that some protections were no longer necessary.

Definition: Affirmative Action

Affirmative action is a government policy which ensures that women and minorities have equal opportunity for jobs, school admissions, and other benefits. Although it was created to prevent discrimination in hiring practices, it has come under fire for *reverse discrimination* against those who aren't minorities.

In the 1978 court case *Regents of the University of California* v. *Bakke*, Allan Bakke claimed he was denied admission to medical school because he was white. The school had a plan in place that set quotas for minority students who could get lower grades, yet be admitted. In a 5-4 decision, the Supreme Court ruled that although the school can consider race as part of the admissions process, *a strict racial quota* violated the Civil Rights Act. Bakke was later admitted.

Definition: Equal Rights Amendment

Women received the right to vote in 1920 with the **Nineteenth Amendment**. It should be noted, that women could vote in certain states before the amendment, as it was up to the states to decide. The amendment merely made all states permit women's suffrage. This is yet another lesson on federalism.

First proposed in 1923, an **Equal Rights Amendment** that ensured equal rights for women under the law passed both the House and Senate in 1972. The amendment was greatly supported by Betty Friedan and the interest group, the **National Organization for Women** (NOW). Although it was close, not enough states ratified it, and it expired in 1982.

Today, women can't be barred from a job based on their gender, nor can states have age requirements that favor men. For example, a state can't have two different legal working ages for men and women. *Title IX* of the Education Amendments of 1972 prevents gender discrimination in educational activities such as sports.

Although women have equality of rights, studies show that they are paid less than men who have similar jobs. In recent decades, strict sexual harassment laws have ensured that women are not discriminated against in the workplace.

Definition: *Roe* v. *Wade*, 1973

Before the Supreme Court handed down this decision, it was up to the states to decide whether a woman could have an abortion or not. *Roe v. Wade* focused on a Texas law which prohibited a woman from having the procedure. In 1973, the Supreme Court supported a woman's right to choose to have an abortion with a 7-2 decision in this case. They ruled that a woman's privacy was protected by the Ninth Amendment's reservation of rights for the people, the Fourth Amendment's right to privacy, and the Fourteenth Amendment's protection of personal liberty. The First and Fifth Amendment were also cited. The decision set the grounds for at what stage a woman can terminate a pregnancy. Overturning this case has been an objective of those who are Right to Life.

Another case regarding the right to privacy was ***Griswold v. Connecticut.*** In this 1965 case, a Connecticut law making it illegal for married people to obtain contraceptives (birth control) was declared unconstitutional by a 7-2 decision. The case was brought by Estelle Griswold, a member of the organization Planned Parenthood. Similar to the *Roe* case, the Bill of Rights was applied to the states with use of the Fourteenth Amendment.

Definition: Don't Ask, Don't Tell (DADT)

In 1993, the official policy for disclosing one's sexuality in the military became ***"don't ask, don't tell."*** It allowed gay and lesbian soldiers to serve, as long as they kept their sexual orientation a secret. However, the end to "don't ask, don't tell" came in 2011. The repeal meant that anyone, regardless of their sexual orientation, could openly serve in the military.

Definition: Defense of Marriage Act (DOMA)

This 1996 law defined marriage as between a man and a woman. Section 3 of this act banned same-sex couples from receiving over a thousand federal benefits such as health insurance and retirement savings. Section 3 was declared unconstitutional in *US* v. *Windsor* in 2013.

Definition: Americans with Disabilities Act (ADA) of 1990

This law protects those with disabilities the same way that the Civil Rights Act of 1964 was meant to protect women and minorities. The act protects those who are qualified for employment, and provides accommodations in public places, restrooms, and on public transportation. As explained earlier, the act has led to unfunded mandates for states to modernize public buses, parks, restrooms, and other facilities.

Question: How does one become a citizen?

If you are born in the United States, you are automatically a citizen. For immigrants, the process to become a citizen is called ***naturalization***. People can qualify for naturalization if they:

1. Have been a permanent resident (green card holder) for 5 years, so long as a person has been present in the US for 30 months. Or, one can be eligible if married for 3 years to a citizen.

2. Are over 18 years old at the time of filing.

3. Are able to read, speak, and write English, and have knowledge of American history and civics/government.

4. Are of good moral character.

NOTE: There are those who are not citizens, yet are living in the country. Some immigrants are without documents and have been referred to as "illegal aliens." They can't vote, though they are required to pay taxes. In recent years, Congress has been working on a process which will provide a path to citizenship for undocumented immigrants.

Review Questions

1. Which form of discrimination did the Twenty-Fourth Amendment outlaw?
    A) Jim Crow laws
    B) School segregation
    C) Poll taxes
    D) Secret ballots
    E) Gender inequality

2. The Supreme Court's decisions in *Reynolds* v. *US* and *Oregon* v. *Smith* involved
    A) declaring segregation unconstitutional
    B) eliminating school prayer in any form
    C) declaring bus segregation unconstitutional
    D) defining the extent of the free exercise clause
    E) establishing rights for those with disabilities

3. Which of the following is NOT a requirement for citizenship?
    A) Must be of good moral character
    B) An understanding of basic lessons in government and civics
    C) Being over 18 years old at the time of filing
    D) Being a permanent resident for 5 years (if single)
    E) Having demonstrated a public act of patriotism

4. *Roe* v. *Wade* and *Griswold* v. *Connecticut* BOTH involved the issue of
    A) abortion
    B) right to privacy
    C) separation of church and state
    D) illegal search and seizure
    E) right to counsel

5. Which of the following would be an example of civil disobedience?
    A) The decision in *Plessy* v. *Ferguson*
    B) Poll taxes
    C) Literacy tests
    D) Sit-ins
    E) Jim Crow laws

6. The Supreme Court's decision in Regents of the *University of California* v. *Bakke* stated that
    A) distinct affirmative action quotas were not justified
    B) a right to privacy was protected
    C) voter precincts can't discriminate
    D) probable cause is needed for searches of homes
    E) rights of the accused must be protected

7. Which of the following NEVER became law at the state or federal level?
    A) Voting Rights Act of 1965
    B) Mississippi Plan
    C) Equal Rights Amendment
    D) Americans with Disabilities Act
    E) Civil Rights Act of 1964

8. The exclusionary rule protects a person's rights because it
    A) prevents illegally seized material from being admitted at a trial
    B) makes the issue of abortion a private matter
    C) allows people of all races to vote
    D) provides a path to citizenship
    E) protects against the establishment of a religion

9. Which of the following is true of free speech?
   A) One can shout fire in a theater
   B) School prayer in public school is protected as free speech
   C) The first amendment can apply to speech that's not spoken
   D) Free speech protects those who create a clear and present danger
   E) Free speech is absolute

10. The Warren Court's landmark decisions have
    A) affirmed separate but equal
    B) expanded rights of the accused
    C) denied citizenship rights
    D) limited the right to privacy
    E) overturned the establishment clause

Free-Response Questions

I. The Bill of Rights became law in 1791, three years after the Constitution was ratified. It defines individual freedoms which some felt needed to be stated directly in the Constitution. Today, however, some of these rights are still being interpreted.

   A. Identify what is meant by selective incorporation. [pp. 86-87]
   B. Choose one of the following cases and explain their impact on the First Amendment.
   - *Schenck* v. *US* [p. 85]
   - *Everson* v. *Board of Education* [p. 86]
   - *Engel* v. *Vitale* [p. 86]

   C. Explain how the court has interpreted right to privacy in one of the following cases.
   - *Roe* v. *Wade* [pp. 90-91]
   - *Griswold* v. *Connecticut* [p. 91]

   D. Choose one of the following cases and explain how the decision utilized an amendment in the Bill of Rights.
   - *Miranda* v. *Arizona* [p. 87]
   - *Gideon* v. *Wainwright* [p. 87]

II. Although the Declaration of Independence stated that all men were created equal, it took a century for that notion to be included into the Constitution. It would take yet another century for everyone's equality to truly be enforced.

   A. Explain the citizenship clause of the Fourteenth Amendment. [p. 86]
   B. Identify two ways in which the Fourteenth and/or Fifteenth Amendment were ignored by Southern states. [pp. 88-89]
   C. Explain how each of the following helped to expand civil rights.
   - *Brown* v. *Board of Education* decision [p. 89]
   - Civil Rights Act of 1964 [p. 89]
   - Voting Rights Act of 1965 [p. 90]

   D. Describe how one other group besides African Americans have gained civil rights since 1960. [pp. 90-91]

Answers and Explanations

1. **C.** The Twenty-Fourth Amendment got rid of poll taxes, or taxes paid to cast a vote.

2. **D.** Both of these cases involved the First Amendment, and the limits of a religion's free exercise.

3. **E.** Proving patriotism is not a requirement for citizenship.

4. **B.** Both cases involved the right to privacy. *Roe* concerned a woman's right to choose to have an abortion. *Griswold* involved the privacy of married couples.

5. **D.** Sit-ins occurred when African Americans sat at the counters at "whites-only" restaurants. It is an example of not obeying laws seen as unjust, or civil disobedience.

6. **A.** Although race can be considered in the admissions process, distinct racial quotas were not justified.

7. **C.** The Equal Rights Amendment for women was proposed by Congress, but 3/4 of the states never ratified it.

8. **A.** The exclusionary rule prevents illegally seized material from being admitted at a trial.

9. **C.** We've seen multiple times that free speech doesn't have to be spoken. Campaign contributions are considered free speech, as well as burning of the flag, as decided in *Texas* v. *Johnson*. In *Tinker* v. *Des Moines*, a student's wardrobe was declared free speech (see No Bull Review Sheet Court Cases Section).

10. **B.** Rights of the accused were expanded for *Gideon* (right to an attorney), *Miranda* (right to remain silent), and *Mapp* (freedom from illegal searches and seizures).

Practice Test One

The AP US Government & Politics Exam contains 60 multiple choice questions, followed by 4 Free-Response Questions (for which you must respond to all 4). The multiple choice section counts for 50% of your score and you have 45 minutes to complete it. You will then have 100 minutes to answer all four essays, which also count for 50% of the score. For the Free-Response Questions, it is encouraged that you use the entire time, and write detailed essays sharing everything that you know relevant to the task.
There is no penalty for wrong guesses, so do not omit multiple choice questions.

1. Who of the following would be most likely to vote along party lines?
    A) Delegate
    B) Partisan
    C) Politico
    D) Trustee
    E) Attitudinal voter

2. Which legislation was responsible for creating an unfunded mandate?
    A) Americans with Disabilities Act
    B) Whistleblower Protection Act
    C) Gulf of Tonkin Resolution
    D) Budget and Impoundment Control Act
    E) Lobbying Disclosure Act

3. Which of the following is NOT an agency of the Executive Branch?
    A) Office of Management and Budget
    B) Federal Trade Commission
    C) General Accounting Office
    D) Office of National Drug Control Policy
    E) Central Intelligence Agency

4. All are true of the Constitution's Great Compromise EXCEPT:
    A) It created a bicameral legislature
    B) The compromise is still in effect today
    C) It gave equal representation to states within the House of Representatives
    D) New Jersey's plan, part of the compromise, provided for equal representation
    E) The Virginia Plan was favored by the more populous states

5. Which of the following is a power reserved for the states?
    A) Amending the Constitution
    B) Ratifying treaties
    C) Running the postal service
    D) Declaration of war
    E) Control of education

6. The purpose of the Bill of Rights was to
    A) appease Federalists who continued to refuse to ratify the Constitution
    B) emphasize the importance of protecting individual rights in the Constitution
    C) guarantee the right to vote to all citizens
    D) increase the power of the Executive Branch
    E) apply the rights of the Constitution to both men and women

7. The *Virginia and Kentucky Resolutions* and the *South Carolina Exposition and Protest* were writings which expressed
   A) the right of factions to expand across the country
   B) the importance of free speech
   C) that a system of checks and balances could not be supported
   D) that states' rights should be respected
   E) that monarchy was an acceptable form of government

8. The "Lemon Test" has been applied to which of the following issues?
   A) Freedom of speech
   B) Free exercise of religion
   C) Search and seizure
   D) Due process for the accused
   E) Federalism

9. What action of Andrew Jackson led to a split in political parties in 1832?
   A) Force Bill
   B) Indian Removal Act
   C) Veto of the Bank of the United States
   D) Signing of the Tariff of 1832
   E) Spoils system

10. The Brady Bill would be most associated with which amendment?
    A) First
    B) Second
    C) Fourth
    D) Fifth
    E) Tenth

11. A female Hispanic voter who is both an advocate for right to life, as well as a proponent for gun control would be considered a
    A) cross-pressured voter
    B) majority-minority voter
    C) organizational voter
    D) critical voter
    E) independent voter

12. Which is a modern-day example of a faction spoken of by James Madison?
    A) House of Representatives
    B) American Medical Association
    C) Congressional Research Service
    D) Joint Chiefs of Staff
    E) Standing Committee Chairman

13. Refer to I-IV below:
    I. Titles of Nobility
    II. Ex post facto laws
    III. Bill of Attainder
    IV. Habeas Corpus

Which of the above would be considered a Denied Power?
   A) I
   B) I and II
   C) I, II, and IV
   D) I, II, and III
   E) I, II, III, and IV

14. Which of the following would be considered part of the unwritten constitution?
    A) Nominating Convention
    B) Electoral College
    C) Elastic Clause
    D) Ratification of treaties
    E) Supreme Court

15. What statement is true regarding minor/third parties?
    A) They have just as good of a chance as major parties to win the Electoral Vote
    B) They are often ideological parties
    C) All third parties must have closed primaries
    D) The Populist Party was the first third party in American History
    E) Third parties can only win office at the federal level, and not within states

16. How can the Legislative Branch best check the Judicial Branch?
    A) Judicial review
    B) Increase the size of the Supreme Court
    C) Cut budgeting for independent regulatory agencies
    D) Appoint justices
    E) Prevent the issuance of writs of certiorari

17. Which of the following is true of PACs?
    A) Only business groups can form PACs
    B) There is no limit to how much money a PAC can contribute to a candidate
    C) Their power decreases as the amount of money an individual can give to a campaign increases
    D) PACs can only be utilized in local elections
    E) PACs have been ruled unconstitutional by the Supreme Court, as a violation of the First Amendment

18. Soft money was reserved for
    A) candidates in local elections
    B) funding block grants
    C) repealing entitlement grants
    D) general political party activities
    E) preventing the impounding of budget funds

19. Which of the following is an example of party polarization?
    A) Expansion of majority-minority districts
    B) Unfunded mandates
    C) Unanimous consent agreements
    D) Logrolling
    E) Split votes along party lines in the House

20. All of these are obstacles that hurt voter turnout EXCEPT:
    A) Apathy
    B) Low trust in government
    C) Open primaries
    D) Depriving felons the right to vote
    E) Mandatory identification cards

21. A poll on gun control might have a large sampling error if
    A) too many people were polled
    B) the poll only contacted registered gun owners
    C) the polling was done via telephone calls
    D) mailings were done randomly
    E) all ethnicities of people were contacted

22. All of the following were true of political machines and municipal bosses of the late nineteenth century EXCEPT:
    A) They aimed to racially integrate government offices
    B) They were often corrupt and took money from the public
    C) Voter fraud was common, as people voted "early and often"
    D) Immigrants were provided with jobs, or money, in exchange for votes
    E) They tended to exist in urban areas

23. Which President would be most likely to favor devolution and New Federalism?
   A) Franklin D. Roosevelt
   B) Barack Obama
   C) Ronald Reagan
   D) John Adams
   E) Theodore Roosevelt

24. A sequester refers to
   A) across-the-board cuts to federal programs
   B) an adjournment of Congress
   C) the raising of the debt-ceiling
   D) a bill that is neither signed or vetoed by the President
   E) the first few months of a President's term

25. A lame duck can refer to
   A) a sitting President who has already been voted out of office
   B) a winner of an election who has not yet had their sophomore surge
   C) the Presidential nominee of a third party
   D) an impeached judge
   E) a President who just had a veto overridden

26. What statement about the Supreme Court is NOT true?
   A) It hears more cases under appellate jurisdiction than it does under original jurisdiction
   B) Justices can be impeached
   C) The court must always use judicial restraint while hearing cases
   D) Justices can view the Constitution as a living document
   E) Very few cases reach the Supreme Court

27. Which of the following is NOT a cabinet position?
   A) Secretary of State
   B) Attorney General
   C) Secretary of the Treasury
   D) Chairman of the Federal Reserve
   E) Secretary of Labor

28. Who would most likely bring about an *amicus curiae* brief?
   A) One looking for a plea bargain
   B) A Senator during an impeachment trial
   C) State courts looking to appeal to the Supreme Court
   D) The Chief Justice of the Supreme Court
   E) An attorney for a special interest group

29. Red tape and duplication are typical complaints about the
   A) House of Representatives
   B) Senate
   C) federal bureaucracy
   D) White House Staff
   E) Supreme Court

30. During the New Deal, the Supreme Court
   A) approved of economic, but not the political issues of Franklin D. Roosevelt
   B) declared several key acts unconstitutional
   C) supported Congress and the President on all forms of legislation
   D) declared Social Security unconstitutional
   E) was increased from nine justices to fourteen

31. The Pendleton Act was instrumental in
   A) giving rights to women
   B) providing civil rights to those with disabilities
   C) reforming civil service
   D) ending the practice of unlimited campaign financing
   E) establishing term limits

32. American foreign policy in the second half of the twentieth century can best be described as
   A) imperialism in the Caribbean
   B) containment in Europe and Asia
   C) noninvolvement
   D) Dollar Diplomacy in China
   E) support for nuclear proliferation in the Middle East

33. What would be an action of the Federal Reserve to make the economy contract?
   A) Cutting interest rates
   B) Buying securities
   C) Decreasing the reserve requirement
   D) Selling of bonds
   E) Decreasing the discount rate

34. Which of the following is NOT a method for proposing or ratifying an amendment?
   A) Proposal by 2/3 of each House
   B) Ratification by 3/4 of the State Legislatures
   C) Congress calling for proposal at a national constitutional convention at request of 2/3 of the states
   D) 3/4 of the states call for a special convention to ratify
   E) Proposal by 3/4 of the state legislatures

35. The decision of *Gibbons* v. *Ogden*
   A) supported the supremacy of the federal government over the states
   B) was the first decision to use judicial review
   C) permitted states to declare acts of the federal government null and void
   D) left issues of interstate commerce up to the President
   E) recognized the importance of honoring contracts

36. The 1964 escalation of the war in Vietnam was a result of the
   A) Domino Theory of Dwight Eisenhower
   B) Gulf of Tonkin Resolution
   C) Nixon Doctrine
   D) Eisenhower Doctrine
   E) War Powers Act

37. The only office where one has to be born in the United States to serve is
   A) President
   B) Senator
   C) Representative
   D) Chief Justice
   E) Secretary of Defense

38. Which Enlightenment philosopher's thoughts on separation of powers were adopted by the Constitution?
   A) John Locke
   B) Voltaire
   C) Baron de Montesquieu
   D) Jean-Jacques Rousseau
   E) Adam Smith

39. Which of the following best describes the actions of civil rights leaders such as Martin Luther King, Jr.?
   A) Encouraging reparations for all citizens who were the children of former slaves
   B) Supporting a mass northern migration of African Americans from the South
   C) Using force to achieve African American equality
   D) De facto, or voluntary, segregation of the races
   E) Disobeying unjust laws of segregation

40. A concurrent power of federalism would be
   A) Education
   B) Taxation
   C) Marriage
   D) Interstate commerce regulation
   E) Postal Service

41. All of the following are entitlements EXCEPT:
   A) Medicaid
   B) Social Security
   C) Supplemental Nutrition Assistance Program (Food Stamps)
   D) Unemployment insurance
   E) Education grants

42. In 1954, the landmark 9-0 *Brown* decision of the Warren Court
   A) limited rights of the accused
   B) limited free speech
   C) desegregated schools
   D) eliminated the power of corporate trusts
   E) deprived the civil liberties of Japanese Americans

43. Which President's use of executive privilege became a Supreme Court issue?
   A) Richard Nixon
   B) Franklin D. Roosevelt
   C) Abraham Lincoln
   D) George W. Bush
   E) Barack Obama

44. Which of the following would be an example of yellow journalism?
   A) Horse-race journalism
   B) Exposing a Presidential scandal
   C) Focusing on racial issues
   D) Exaggerating and sensationalizing issues
   E) Only reporting on one candidate's platform

45. Which is NOT traditionally considered to be part of the iron triangle?
   A) Congressional committee
   B) Federal judge
   C) Bureaucratic agency
   D) Lobbyist
   E) Interest Group

46. Presidents Ronald Reagan and Jimmy Carter were similar in that both
   A) attempted to rescue American hostages from Iran
   B) supported a policy of détente
   C) were not part of Washington, DC politics before being elected
   D) supported the theory of "trickle down" economics
   E) negotiated treaties between Israel and Egypt

47. In *Dred Scott* v. *Sandford*, the Supreme Court ruled that
   A) the Missouri Compromise was constitutional
   B) slaves were property and couldn't sue in court
   C) runaway slaves could be compensated for lost wages
   D) slavery was unconstitutional
   E) the rights of the accused must be protected

48. How is reapportionment determined?
   A) Bipartisan legislation
   B) Joint resolution
   C) A census is taken every ten years
   D) Concurrent resolution
   E) *Stare decisis*

49. How can gerrymandering help out a political party?
   A) It can force PACs to give money to campaigns
   B) If one member of Congress votes for someone's bill, that person will reciprocate
   C) It can lead to greater control of the House of Representatives
   D) It can go around seniority and lead to more chairs in standing committees
   E) More Senators can be awarded to states through gerrymandering

50. Pork-barrel legislation typically benefits
   A) northern states
   B) only certain districts
   C) southern states
   D) Presidential candidates
   E) members of the Rules Committee

51. ***"The power to tax involves the power to destroy"***
   The above quote is most associated with what Supreme Court decision by John Marshall?
   A) *Marbury* v. *Madison*
   B) *Gibbons* v. *Ogden*
   C) *McCulloch* v. *Maryland*
   D) *Worcester* v. *Georgia*
   E) *Dartmouth* v. *Woodward*

52. Which committee has been referred to as the "traffic cop" of the House?
   A) Ways and Means
   B) Appropriations
   C) Armed Services
   D) Budget
   E) Rules

53. The Speaker of the House is chosen by the
   A) President
   B) members of the House
   C) Conference Chair
   D) Majority and Minority whips
   E) constituents of the states

54. Which of the following is a specific power of the Senate?
   A) Putting a bill in a hopper
   B) Deciding a deadlocked Presidential Election
   C) Ratifying treaties
   D) Starting revenue bills
   E) Serving a two year term

55. Use of the franking privilege would include
   A) redrawing federal district lines
   B) receiving a pension after retirement
   C) getting a state car and fuel credit card
   D) sending out mail to constituents
   E) securing office space in the Capitol

56. One former power of Congress that was found unconstitutional was use of
   A) logrolling
   B) earmarks
   C) the legislative veto
   D) riders
   E) pork-barrel legislation

57. Which statement is true about the American government today?
   A) Political party bosses have never before been so powerful
   B) The influence of special interests has declined over the last few decades
   C) The size of the bureaucracy is smaller today than it was in 1933
   D) The media has little-to-no impact on local politics
   E) In recent years, more minorities have become delegates in primaries

58. Which of the following is NOT a way in which the electoral process has become more democratic since the founding of the nation?
   A) Primary Elections
   B) Lifting restrictions of property ownership for voting
   C) Nominating conventions
   D) Literacy tests
   E) Ratification of the Seventeenth Amendment

59. The highest ranking White House Staff advisor is the
   A) Secretary of State
   B) Joint Chiefs of Staff
   C) Chief of Staff
   D) Deputy Chief of Staff
   E) Press Secretary

60. *Plessy* v. *Ferguson* affirmed which of the following?
   A) Separate but equal was constitutional
   B) The Civil Rights Act of 1866 was unconstitutional
   C) Jim Crow laws were unconstitutional
   D) Schools in Kansas could be segregated with the consent of the people
   E) The Due Process clause of the Fourteenth Amendment made all segregation unconstitutional

Free-Response Questions

I. Citizens have the ability to take part in the political process. Though not directly legislating as members of Congress, the average citizen can be very active in how policy is created.

   A. Explain three factors that can affect a person's ideology. [pp. 19-21]

   B. Identify two ways that a citizen can be politically active. [pp. 22-23]

   C. Define two of the following, and indicate how they allow average citizens to be part of the political process.[p. 49]
- Initiative
- Referendum
- Recall

   D. Describe one requirement needed when running for the following three offices. [p. 8]
- House of Representatives
- Senator
- President

II. Throughout United States history, specific acts have limited potential tyranny within the government.

   A. Describe one of the following acts, and illustrate how it has limited the power of the President.
- Budget and Impoundment Control Act [p. 77]
- War Powers Act [p. 56]

   B. Describe one of the following acts, and illustrate how it has limited the power of the bureaucracy.
- Pendleton Act [p. 75]
- Freedom of Information Act [p. 87]

   C. Describe two of the following acts, and illustrate how they protect rights of individuals.
- Americans with Disabilities Act [p. 91]
- Civil Rights Act of 1964 [pp. 89-90]
- Voting Rights Act of 1965 [p. 90]

III. The Supreme Court has handed down decisions that have affected every walk of life in America. From social issues, to political decisions, their renderings have been accepted as law, and have changed the way people live.

   A. Identify the role of *stare decisis* in the judicial process. [p. 69]

   B. Explain the relevance of citizenship in two of the following decisions.
- *Dred Scott* v. *Sandford* [p. 88]
- *Plessy* v. *Ferguson* [p. 88]
- *Brown* v. *Board of Education* [p. 89]

   C. Identify the Court's decision in two of the following, and explain if rights were expanded or limited.
- *Regents of the University of California* v. *Bakke* [p. 90]
- *Reynolds* v. *US* [p. 86]
- *Miranda* v. *Arizona* [p. 87]

IV. Power is not always evenly distributed throughout the government, as at different times in United States history, the President has been stronger than Congress. In other generations, Congress has limited the President's power.

   A. Describe two of the following ways in which a President can expand power.
- Veto [pp. 44-45]
- Executive Order [p. 56]
- Executive Privilege [pp. 59-60]

   B. Explain how Congress has used two of the following in its history to expand power.
- Legislative Veto [p. 46]
- Budgeting [pp. 49, 77-78]
- Impeachment [p. 42]

   C. Describe how the President and Congress worked together for a common purpose in two of the following periods.
- New Deal [pp. 69, 75-76]
- Cold War [p. 79]
- War on Terror [pp. 56, 79]

Answers and Explanations

Score Estimate for Multiple Choice:
26 correct = 2
37 correct = 3
46 correct = 4
53 correct = 5

1. **B**. One who votes along party lines is called a partisan. Sometimes the two major parties work together for *bipartisanship*.

2. **A**. The Americans with Disabilities Act created unfunded mandates, as states have to provide accommodations for public facilities such as buses, restrooms, and parks.

3. **C**. The GAO is a staff agency of Congress that investigates how the government spends federal dollars.

4. **C**. The House of Representatives is based on population. States with greater populations have more representatives. The Senate has equal representation.

5. **E**. Education, driving, drinking, and marriage laws are examples of issues that are reserved for the states.

6. **B**. The Bill of Rights, added in 1791, was an appeal to Anti-Federalists who believed the Constitution would infringe upon individual rights. The Bill of Rights came *after* the Constitution was ratified.

7. **D**. John C. Calhoun's *South Carolina Exposition and Protest* said that states should be able to declare acts of Congress "null and void." This was similar to what Thomas Jefferson and James Madison wrote in their Kentucky and Virginia Resolutions.

8. **B**. The decision of *Lemon* v. *Kurtzman* created the "Lemon Test" where a government's laws had to be secular, not affect or inhibit religion, and had to prevent entanglements with religion.

9. **C**. Issues with the national bank caused the first two major party splits in American History. The split in the 1830s led to the formation of the Whig Party.

10. **B**. The Brady Bill looked to expand background checks to those purchasing firearms.

11. **A**. A cross-pressured voter might have several conflicting ideologies. They can be liberal on some issues, yet conservative on others.

12. **B**. The AMA is an interest group, or modern-day faction.

13. **D**. *Habeas corpus* involves a right to due process and a fair trial. It can be suspended by the President in a time of war.

14. **A**. Though it is common procedure to have one every four years, nominating conventions are not mentioned in the Constitution.

15. **B**. Third parties are often ideological parties, who rather than value winning, are more concerned with getting their view heard.

16. **B**. Congress can change the size of the Supreme Court. The President can then appoint justices.

17. **C**. As the amount of money an individual can give to a campaign goes up, the power of the PAC decreases. Recently there has been a boost to individual limits.

18. **D**. Before the Bipartisan Campaign Reform Act, a large amount of soft money was given to political parties for general purposes. Of course, those general purposes ultimately helped candidates indirectly.

19. **E**. Party polarization occurs when political parties are divided, and can't get along in Congress.

20. **C**. Open primaries actually help voter turnout. Closed primaries prevent non-registered party members from voting.

21. **B**. A poll needs to be fair, and open to all ideas. Contacting only gun owners for a poll on gun control would lead to unreliable results.

22. **A**. Political bosses such as Boss Tweed of Tammany Hall were not concerned with racial integration. The other choices were all associated with political machines. Political bosses were known for municipal (city) corruption.

23. **C**. Ronald Reagan supported decreasing the federal workforce, and returning some powers to the states. This is called devolution, and is a part of New Federalism.

24. **A**. Sequesters are terrible pills to swallow for the government, as cuts occur across nearly the entire government.

25. **A**. A lame duck has lost much of their political power, as they are leaving office in a matter of months. They were either just voted out, or their term is ending.

26. **C**. In addition to judicial restraint, justices can also be active. Judicial activism is the belief that the Supreme Court should rely on its personal views and be active in addressing social and political issues and policies.

27. **D**. The Chairman of the Federal Reserve is an independent position outside of the cabinet.

28. **E**. *Amicus curiae* means "a friend of the court," and is a brief from a person who believes they have information that is useful for the court's evaluation of a case. *Amicus curiae* briefs are often used by special interest groups.

29. **C**. These are complaints of the very large, and very specified, federal bureaucracy.

30. **B**. Congress and the President were on the same page, but not the Supreme Court. *Schechter Poultry Corporation* v. *US* led to the end of the National Industrial Recovery Act. *US* v. *Butler* struck down the Agricultural Adjustment Act. Both were important pieces of the New Deal.

31. **C**. The Pendleton Act helped to end the patronage system where government jobs were awarded to political supporters. Today, the merit system determines government employment.

32. **B**. From 1945-1991, US foreign policy was dominated by stopping the spread of communism. This was known as containment.

33. **D**. When the Fed sells bonds, money supply decreases and the economy contracts. When the Fed buys bonds, money supply increases and more spending occurs.

34. **E**. Amendments can be *ratified* by 3/4 of the state legislatures, but can't be proposed by 3/4 of them.

35. **A**. In the *Gibbons* case, federal licenses, not ones issued by the states, proved to be superior regarding interstate commerce.

36. **B**. The Gulf of Tonkin Resolution gave President Johnson a "blank check" as Commander-in-chief of the Vietnam conflict. This meant an escalation of the use of ground troops.

37. **A**. To be President, one must be born in the United States.

38. **C**. Baron de Montesquieu's Enlightenment thought influenced the US government's three branches of government, or separation of powers.

39. **E**. Civil disobedience involved many activities, including *freedom rides* on integrated buses and *sit-ins* at segregated restaurants.

40. **B**. A concurrent power is shared between both federal and state governments. Taxation is a concurrent power, as both entities can tax.

41. **E**. Entitlements are grants which give income to families or individuals. It can be in the form of welfare financial support and Medicaid health insurance for low-income Americans, as well as Social Security and Medicare for older citizens.

42. **C**. In the 9-0 decision of *Brown* v. *Board of Education of Topeka, Kansas*, school segregation was declared unconstitutional, as "separate but equal" was inherently unequal.

43. **A**. The court ruled in *US* v. *Nixon* that President Richard Nixon was not protected by executive privilege, and had to hand over tape-recordings. Nixon remains the only President to resign from office.

44. **D**. Yellow journalism occurred prior to the Spanish American War, as inaccurate and sensational journalism swayed public opinion against Spain.

45. **B**. A federal judge would not be typical in an iron triangle, as it would traditionally only include agencies, special interests, and Congress.

46. **C**. Carter was a peanut farmer and Governor of Georgia, and Reagan was an actor and Governor of California. Voters usually see Washington outsiders as a welcome change to "politics as usual."

47. **B**. The Court ruled against Dred Scott, saying that slaves were property, and people could not be denied property. The Fourteenth Amendment overturned the case.

48. **C**. Every ten years, a census, or detailed population count, is taken. Once the populations of the states are known, the number of representatives each state has can be determined.

49. **C**. It's in the interest of the state's party in power to increase their number or representatives. To do this, they draw lines in wacky asymmetrical ways, so that they can create districts which they know they can politically control. This is gerrymandering.

50. **B**. Pork involves laws that benefit only certain districts, usually in the form of public works projects such as bridges or roads. The idea is to bring money into certain areas and benefit specific representatives.

51. **C**. John Marshall's decisions generally increased the power of the federal government. For example, in *McCulloch* v. *Maryland*, he said that Maryland could not tax the Bank of the United States.

52. **E**. The Rules Committee determines under what circumstances bills can come to the floor in the House.

53. **B**. The Speaker of the House is chosen by the other representatives, and almost certainly is a member of the majority party.

54. **C**. The Senate ratifies treaties and confirms appointments. The rest of the choices are unique to the House of Representatives.

55. **D**. This postage perk is called the franking privilege. It allows incumbents to use stationery and postage for "communication," that often turns into "campaigning."

56. **C**. Declared unconstitutional in 1983, the legislative veto gave Congress the power to put provisions into laws permitting them to negate some decisions made by the President or Executive agencies. In essence, this gave the Legislative Branch veto power over executive decisions.

57. **E**. In recent years, more women and minorities have become delegates, cabinet officials, Supreme Court justices, and members of Congress.

58. **D**. Literacy tests looked to discriminate and prevent African Americans from voting.

59. **C**. The Chief of Staff is highest ranking Presidential advisor in the White House.

60. **A**. *Plessy* v. *Ferguson* is the opposite of *Brown* v. *Board of Education*. In Plessy, "separate but equal" was seen as constitutional. This meant that as long as blacks and whites had the same type of facilities, they could be separate. *Brown* reversed that in 1954.

Practice Test Two

The AP US Government & Politics Exam contains 60 multiple choice questions, followed by 4 Free-Response Questions (for which you must respond to all 4). The multiple choice section counts for 50% of your score and you have 45 minutes to complete it. You will then have 100 minutes to answer all four essays, which also count for 50% of the score. For the Free-Response Questions, it is encouraged that you use the entire time, and write detailed essays sharing everything that you know relevant to the task.
There is no penalty for wrong guesses, so do not omit multiple choice questions.

1. Majoritarianism is most associated with
    A) Monarchy
    B) Dictatorship
    C) Communism
    D) Democracy
    E) Oligarchy

2. Shays' Rebellion exposed which weakness of the Articles of Confederation?
    A) Lack of an army
    B) Failure to regulate interstate commerce
    C) Inability to collect taxes
    D) Lack of a Postal Service
    E) A weak central court system

3. George Washington set a precedent in foreign policy by advocating
    A) imperialistic opportunities in the Western Hemisphere
    B) annexation of land in the Pacific northwest
    C) avoiding alliances with foreign nations
    D) protecting American naval rights in the Mediterranean
    E) removal of Native Americans to west of the Mississippi River

4. The Fifth Amendment resolves that the rights of life, liberty, and property cannot be denied to any person without due process of law. Which amendment applied due process to the states?
    A) First
    B) Eighth
    C) Fourteenth
    D) Sixth
    E) Thirteenth

5. Refer to the following:
    I. Bill of Rights
    II. Articles of Confederation
    III. Declaration of Independence
    IV. Constitution

Which of the above contained specific rules and laws which had to be followed by the government?
    A) I and IV
    B) I, II, and IV
    C) I, II, III
    D) I, II, III, IV
    E) II and IV

6. The Virginia Plan can best be seen today in the configuration of the
   A) Senate
   B) Supreme Court
   C) Bureaucracy
   D) Executive Office of the President
   E) House of Representatives

7. Which is true about raising revenue in the United States?
   A) The government can tax imports, but not exports
   B) Taxation is determined by a flat tax
   C) The Federal Reserve can increase taxes
   D) Taxation can only be done on federal levels
   E) Only a small percentage of taxes go to entitlement programs

8. Which of the following is a Constitutional requirement to be a Supreme Court justice?
   A) Must be 30 years old
   B) Have to be a permanent resident of the country for 30 years
   C) Need to pass a civil service test
   D) Must have been an associate justice for three years
   E) There are no requirements in the Constitution

9. In what type of government are decisions made at the top with less regard for the common citizen?
   A) Pluralist
   B) Elitist
   C) Majoritarian
   D) Direct Democracy
   E) Representative Democracy

10. Political socialization is important because it helps political scientists measure
    A) exit polling
    B) how an ideology develops
    C) apathy in the political process
    D) party polarization
    E) voter registration trends

Use these speakers to answer questions 11-13

Speaker 1: "A woman has the right to choose to have an abortion. A woman has a right to privacy."

Speaker 2: "The economy would thrive if the government would stop interfering with the free market."

Speaker 3: "The Second Amendment gives everyone the right to carry a firearm at all times. Gun-control laws prevent law-abiding citizens from owning guns. Criminals won't obey the law anyway."

Speaker 4: "Health care should not be a privilege, it should be a right."

Speaker 5: "Although I believe that entitlements should not be cut, I also feel that my taxes should not go up every year."

11. Which speaker would support the decision of *Roe* v. *Wade*?
    A) Speaker 1
    B) Speaker 2
    C) Speaker 3
    D) Speaker 4
    E) Speaker 5

12. Which combination of speakers would most likely vote for the Democratic Party?
    A) Speakers 1 and 2
    B) Speakers 3 and 4
    C) Speakers 2 and 5
    D) Speakers 1 and 4
    E) Speakers 3 and 5

13. Which of the above speakers would campaign commercials target the most?
    A) Speaker 1
    B) Speaker 2
    C) Speaker 3
    D) Speaker 4
    E) Speaker 5

14. Who is most likely to vote in an upcoming election?
    A) 18 year-old female who just graduated high school
    B) 25 year-old naturalized citizen
    C) 30 year-old female with three kids
    D) 35 year-old male with high school degree
    E) 60 year-old college graduate

15. What impact does a party-column ballot have?
    A) It discourages people from voting for all offices
    B) Often, the party ballot leads to ticket-splitting
    C) Exit polls are unreliable when party-column ballots are used
    D) A straight-ticket supporting one political party for all offices often occurs
    E) Discrimination can occur, as these ballots are never translated for those who need it

16. What event in American History resulted in the alignment of African Americans, labor leaders, and workers with the Democratic Party?
    A) Civil War
    B) Reconstruction
    C) Reaganomics
    D) New Deal
    E) Ratification of Constitution

17. Protection from unreasonable search and seizure was relevant to which Supreme Court case?
    A) *Mapp* v. *Ohio*
    B) *Miranda* v. *Arizona*
    C) *Schenck* v. *US*
    D) *Buckley* v. *Valeo*
    E) *Baker* v. *Carr*

18. Which of the following is true of the Presidential Election?
    A) The person who wins the popular vote always wins the election
    B) The candidate who wins a plurality of a state's votes, wins all of the state's electors
    C) The people vote directly for the Presidential candidate
    D) The President and Vice President are on separate ballots
    E) Candidates campaign equally in all states

19. Interest groups differ from political parties, as interest groups
    A) don't try to control legislation
    B) aren't concerned with elections
    C) focus on a narrow range of issues
    D) can't fundraise
    E) are found in the Constitution

20. A corporate lobbyist would be very interested in supporting
   A) labor unions
   B) civil rights
   C) laissez-faire
   D) a safe environment
   E) entitlement programs

21. Lobbyists must do all of the following EXCEPT
   A) register
   B) obey campaign finance laws
   C) put limits on excessive gifts
   D) disclose financial activities in reports
   E) be a member of a PAC

22. A major social movement in United States history was
   A) the New Deal
   B) the Constitutional Convention
   C) Shays' Rebellion
   D) the Civil Rights Era
   E) the Cold War

23. A prime objective of the Tea Party Movement is to
   A) permit the inclusion of school prayer
   B) increase entitlement programs
   C) limit government spending
   D) increase taxes on the wealthy
   E) put limits on firearm ammunition clips

24. What special interest group would most frequently focus on the Justice Department?
   A) American Medical Association
   B) American Association of Retired Persons
   C) American Civil Liberties Union
   D) Chamber of Commerce
   E) National Association of Manufacturers

25. All of the following are ways that pro-union interest groups can raise money EXCEPT:
   A) Tariffs
   B) Foundation Grants
   C) Dues
   D) Donations
   E) Fundraiser

26. How does a PAC differ from a Super PAC?
   A) A Super PAC is used in a Presidential Election
   B) PACs are used only at the state level
   C) Only a Super PAC can be a 527
   D) Only a Super PAC can be a 501(c)(4)
   E) PACs can't be considered an "independent expenditure"

27. An example of checks and balances would be
   A) Congress overriding a Presidential veto
   B) the President sending military aid to Europe
   C) the federal government coining money
   D) the Vice President presiding over the Senate
   E) a filibuster in the Senate

28. There was bipartisanship support for
   A) the impeachment of Bill Clinton
   B) the Affordable Care Act
   C) passage of the Campaign Reform Act of 2002
   D) the filibuster against the Civil Rights Act
   E) a sequester in 2013

29. Alexander Hamilton's national bank was passed
   A) with the help of the Elastic Clause
   B) after a joint session of Congress and the Supreme Court
   C) as a compromise which moved the nation's capital to Philadelphia
   D) as part of the Treaty of Paris
   E) after an override of President Washington's veto

30. What form of media were muckrakers traditionally known for using?
   A) Radio
   B) Magazines
   C) Television
   D) Internet
   E) Speeches

31. Who of the following would be LEAST likely to use the media to convey their personal agenda?
   A) President
   B) Speaker of the House
   C) Supreme Court justice
   D) State governor
   E) Vice President

32. What type of story would get the most scrutiny during a Presidential Campaign?
   A) Historical policies of the candidate
   B) Plans for relieving unemployment
   C) The latest Election Day poll
   D) Foreign policy stances
   E) A comparison of party platforms on social issues

33. Coining money and fixing the standards of weights and measures are powers of the
   A) Treasury Department
   B) Executive Office of the President
   C) Legislative Branch
   D) Federal Reserve Board
   E) President

34. Who of the following has the shortest term in office?
   A) President
   B) Chief Justice
   C) Majority Leader of the Senate
   D) Speaker of the House
   E) Vice President

35. Marginal districts would be ones that
   A) are controlled by Democrats
   B) are controlled by Independents
   C) have a large number of minority constituents
   D) are controlled by Republicans
   E) typically feature tight elections

36. In a Presidential Election
   A) certain states receive more attention from both candidates
   B) every state has an equal say in the outcome
   C) people vote for the Presidential candidates directly
   D) the popular vote determines the election
   E) less money is spent in swing states

37. Democrats were strongest in Congress during the
   A) 1920s
   B) 2010s
   C) 1870s
   D) 1930s
   E) 1790s

38. Who would be LEAST likely to caucus together in Congress?
   A) African Americans
   B) Those seeking earmarks
   C) Environmentalists
   D) Hispanic Americans
   E) Those who support a similar interest group

39. Which Congressional staff agency is a part of the Library of Congress?
   A) Congressional Budget Office
   B) General Accounting Office
   C) Congressional Research Service
   D) Central Intelligence Agency
   E) Permanent Select Committee on Intelligence

40. An example of legislative oversight would be
   A) passing a law for road construction in the states
   B) fixing mistakes made by a federal agency
   C) proposing an amendment
   D) filibustering an undesired bill
   E) cutting off funding for state entitlement programs

41. What type of committee would be used to compromise different versions of a bill in both the House and Senate?
   A) Conference
   B) Standing
   C) Joint
   D) Special
   E) Ways and Means

42. The "graying" of America has led to problems within the
   A) Federal Deposit Insurance Corporation
   B) Social Security fund
   C) Reconstruction Finance Corporation
   D) Federal Reserve's monetary policy
   E) Federal Emergency Relief Administration

43. A closed rule
   A) prevents introduction of amendments to a bill
   B) limits earmarks to those with high seniority
   C) outlaws logrolling on a bill
   D) encourages pork-barrel legislation
   E) can only be done on Constitutional amendment proposals

44. What statement is true regarding vetoes?
   A) Most bills are vetoed
   B) A veto can be overridden by 3/4 of the legislature
   C) The President can't use a line-item veto
   D) If the President doesn't sign a bill, it can't become law
   E) There are limits as to how many times a President can use veto power in a year

45. The purpose of a filibuster is to
   A) delay a measure as long as possible
   B) pass a bill that is for the public good
   C) prevent the President from signing a bill
   D) violate unanimous consent agreements
   E) protest against germaneness requirements

46. In *Federalist #10*, James Madison argued that
   A) a large republic could never successfully exist
   B) the Electoral College would protect the voting rights of all
   C) all men were created equal with unalienable rights
   D) the Articles of Confederation could succeed if there was a stronger army
   E) tyranny of factions could be controlled in a large republic

47. Governors in some states can be removed from office in a procedure called
   A) Referendum
   B) Vote of confidence
   C) Recall
   D) Initiative
   E) Solidary incentive

48. A liberal Presidential candidate looking to balance the ticket, would most likely choose a Vice President who is
   A) Ultra-liberal
   B) Moderate
   C) Libertarian
   D) Ultra-conservative
   E) Socialist

49. Which Amendment calls for a two-term limit for the Presidency?
   A) Twenty-First
   B) Twenty-Second
   C) Twenty-Third
   D) Twenty-Fourth
   E) Twenty-Fifth

50. A provision of the War Powers Act
   A) prevents the President from ever deploying forces to Asia
   B) eliminates cuts to military funding
   C) requires Senate approval before constructing nuclear weapons
   D) prevents the President from impounding funds
   E) requires Congressional approval for lengthy military operations

51. Which is true about the history of the Presidency?
   A) The President has always been stronger than Congress
   B) Using executive privilege is always acceptable
   C) President Abraham Lincoln vetoed more bills than any other President in history
   D) Presidents have vetoed more bills than they have signed
   E) The power of the President has increased since World War II

52. Ad hoc structure of the White House Staff would involve
   A) only the Chief of Staff reporting directly to the President
   B) less than ten, but more than five, assistants reporting to the President
   C) task forces, advisors, committees, and small groups reporting to the President
   D) groups reporting to the Vice President, who then speaks to the President
   E) no one reporting to the President except for the members of the cabinet

53. Which president appointed the first female justice to the Supreme Court?
   A) Jimmy Carter
   B) Ronald Reagan
   C) George H.W. Bush
   D) Bill Clinton
   E) George W. Bush

54. In *Marbury* v. *Madison*, Chief Justice John Marshall
   A) used the principle of judicial review
   B) upheld the constitutionality of the Judiciary Act of 1789
   C) voiced strong misgivings to the creation of a national bank
   D) denied states the right to make contracts
   E) struck down a fraudulent purchase of land near the Yazoo River

55. Refer to the following:
   I. *Miranda* v. *Arizona*
   II. *Roe* v. *Wade*
   III. *Brown* v. *Board of Education*
   IV. *Gideon* v. *Wainwright*

   Which of the above cases expanded rights of the accused?
   A) I and II
   B) II and III
   C) I, II, and IV
   D) I and IV
   E) I, II, III, and IV

56. All of the following are true about judicial procedures EXCEPT
   A) Most criminal cases are plea bargained
   B) An attorney must have a good standing to sue
   C) Class action suits can be brought by multiple people
   D) Writs of certiorari are generously granted by the Supreme Court
   E) "Friends of the court" can submit briefs

57. An example of a government corporation is the
   A) Environmental Protection Agency
   B) Post Office
   C) Security and Exchange Commission
   D) Federal Communications Commission
   E) Federal Trade Commission

58. All of the following are unconstitutional EXCEPT:
   A) Bill of Attainder
   B) De facto segregation
   C) Ex post facto laws
   D) Literacy tests
   E) Poll taxes

59. What changes most often in the national budget?
   A) Discretionary spending
   B) Monetary policy
   C) Entitlement spending
   D) Mandatory spending
   E) Reserve requirements

60. What does the "wall of separation" refer to?
   A) Distance between the President and the people
   B) Red tape within the bureaucracy
   C) Political polarization in Congress
   D) Gap between the rich and the poor
   E) Separation of Church and State

Free-Response Questions

I. By establishing a system of checks and balances, the framers of the Constitution were able to prevent one branch of government from becoming too strong. However, confrontation soon emerged concerning public policy and agendas.
   A. Explain separation of powers. [p. 8]
   B. Give two examples of how the Legislative Branch can check the Executive and/or Judicial branches. [pp. 12-13]
   C. Give two examples of how the Executive Branch can check the Legislative and/or Judicial branches. [pp. 12-13]
   D. Give two examples of how the powers of the federal bureaucracy can be checked. [p. 76]

II. Amendments have been added to the Constitution to protect the rights of average citizens. However, today those amendments and freedoms are still being interpreted by the United States judicial system.
   A. Describe the relationship between the following amendments and individual liberties. [pp. 85-86]
      - First
      - Fifth
      - Fourteenth
   B. Explain how the Supreme Court protected rights in two of the following cases.
      - *Buckley* v. *Valeo* [p. 34]
      - *Mapp* v. *Ohio* [p. 87]
      - *Griswold* v. *Connecticut* [p. 91]
   C. Explain the relationship between selective incorporation and the Bill of Rights. [pp. 86-87]

III. In drafting a Constitution, it was decided that a strong federal government should exist in the United States. However, the extent of states' rights continued to be debated for decades.
   A. Define federalism. [p. 9]
   B. Indicate two delegated/enumerated powers of Congress. [p. 9]
   C. Indicate two reserved powers of the states. [p. 9]
   D. Describe the role John Marshall had in defining federal powers during the early years of the United States. [pp. 11-12]

IV. Many different people have a say in the policy-making process. Between special interests, agencies, Congress, and the President, there are a lot of eyes looking over how laws and regulations are enforced.
- A. Define Pluralism [pp. 13-14]
- B. Identify two ways in which special interests can affect public policy. [pp. 31-33]
- C. Explain how both of the following affect the policy-making process.
    - Independent Regulatory Agencies [pp. 57-59]
    - Legislative oversight [p. 59]
- D. Describe one monetary policy of the Federal Reserve that can cause inflation. [pp. 76-77]

Answers and Explanations

Score Estimate for Multiple Choice:
26 correct = 2
37 correct = 3
46 correct = 4
53 correct = 5

1. **D.** Decisions in a democracy are influenced by majority rule, or where actions reflect the opinions of the majority. Although majoritarianism might lead some to fear a "tyranny of the majority," the Constitution looks to ensure the rights of all.

2. **A.** A lack of a national army meant that Shays' Rebellion could not be put down efficiently. The uprising was enough to convince many that a stronger Constitution was needed.

3. **C.** George Washington established the foreign policy precedent of neutrality.

4. **C.** The Fourteenth Amendment applied due process of law to the states.

5. **B.** Although the Declaration of Independence outlined liberties, the document did not have the force of law behind it.

6. **E.** James Madison wanted a bicameral (2 house) legislature based on population. The greater the population, the more representatives a state would have.

7. **A.** The Commercial Compromise gave the federal government the power to tax imports but not exports. A tax on imports is referred to as a tariff.

8. **E.** There are no requirements in the Constitution for becoming a Supreme Court Justice.

9. **B.** In Elitism, the decisions are made at the top with less regard for the common citizen. Master politicians and property owners are the ones in charge, as decisions are made with less regard for public opinion.

10. **B.** The study of how ideology is passed from one generation to another is called political socialization. Of all of the factors that shape this process, such as school, media, life experience, and peers, parents have the greatest influence.

11. **A.** The decision in *Roe* v. *Wade* defended a woman's right to have an abortion.

12. **D.** Speaker 1 is pro-choice, and Speaker 4 favors universal health care. Both are traditionally liberal beliefs.

13. **E.** Speaker 5 is a moderate, and might be undecided. Or, Speaker 5 could be an independent. Finally, Speaker 5 is a cross-pressured voter, where different issues in their life sway their ideology.

14. **E.** Studies show that older Americans, as well as those with more education, tend to be more active in politics. They also vote more often.

15. **D.** Party-column ballots separate all of the offices into columns based on the political party. Therefore, one could merely choose one column and vote a *straight ticket* for one party.

16. **D**. Franklin D. Roosevelt's New Deal attracted more liberals, African Americans, women, economists, and union leaders to the Democratic Party in the 1930s.

17. **A**. *Mapp* v. *Ohio* led to protections against illegal searches and seizures.

18. **B**. Whoever wins the plurality, or the most votes in a state, takes all of that state's Electoral Votes. It's not the majority (more than half)… it's the plurality. If there are three popular candidates, a majority would be quite difficult to obtain.

19. **C**. Unlike a political party which has a wide range of objectives, special interest groups are usually concerned with only one or a few issues.

20. **C**. A corporate lobbyist would look out for the interests of large corporations. Decreasing regulation and fostering laissez-faire would be goals of such a lobbyist.

21. **E**. Not every lobbyist has to be involved with Political Action Committees, or raising campaign funds.

22. **D**. Social movements reshape culture. The Civil Rights Era did just that.

23. **C**. The Tea Party Movement aims to lower taxes and reduce government spending.

24. **C**. The ACLU (American Civil Liberties Union) defends liberty and the rights of all people. The Justice Department makes sure that there is adequate protection of citizen rights in terms of criminal activity, and consumer exploitation.

25. **A**. Tariffs are federal taxes on imports. That's not a method for interest groups to raise money.

26. **E**. As an "independent expenditure," Super PACs can spend as much money as they want, so long as the money isn't directly connected to a candidate or political party… hence, why it's an *independent* expenditure.

27. **A**. Congress can check the President's veto by overriding it with a 2/3 vote.

28. **C**. Also known as the McCain-Feingold Act, the Bipartisan Campaign Reform Act changed the way that campaigns can be financed.

29. **A**. The National Bank is not in the Constitution, but Congress used the Elastic Clause, as it felt that the Bank was "necessary and proper."

30. **B**. Muckrakers were journalists who wrote books and magazine articles c1900. Their writings helped lead to progressive reforms for workers and consumers.

31. **C**. Supreme Court media interviews are rare, but they do occur. These interviews are often biographical or general.

32. **C**. This is called *horse-race journalism*. In Presidential Campaigns, the media spends so much time on polls, debates, candidates' life stories, image, and gaffe sound-bites (mess-ups), that they often overlook what's at stake.

33. **C**. Congress has the power to coin money and fix the standards of weights and measures.

34. **D**. All representatives, including the Speaker of the House, are elected to a two-year term.

35. **E**. Marginal districts are those where there are tight elections. Safe districts are those where the incumbent overwhelmingly wins.

36. **A**. Presidential candidates concentrate their campaign efforts on certain states, usually the swing states.

37. **D**. Franklin D. Roosevelt's New Deal had overwhelming support from a Democratic Congress.

38. **B**. Earmarks (part of a spending bill which allocates money for something specific) aren't popular in the public eye. Though they are used, it's very unlikely members of Congress would openly caucus for them.

39. **C**. A part of the Library of Congress (the government's book, media, and copyright headquarters), the CRS provides policy and legal analysis to committees and members of Congress.

40. **B**. If Congress believes bad decisions are being made, or mistakes have occurred, they can step in and hold agencies accountable for missteps. The main purpose is to make sure that government workers are doing what they are supposed to be doing.

41. **A**. Conference committees are temporary ones that look to find a compromise between House and Senate versions of the same bill.

42. **B**. As Baby Boomers get older, or grayer, the Social Security fund could face serious obstacles.

43. **A**. A closed rule in the House means that there is limited debate, and a refusal to introduce amendments.

44. **C**. Most states have a line-item veto, as governors can choose which parts of a bill are vetoed. However the President does not have this luxury.

45. **A**. A Filibuster is an unlimited debate of a bill. It's done to delay a measure with hopes that it won't pass. It can only take place in the Senate, and is exercised by those who believe they will lose a vote.

46. **E**. Madison believed that factions could be controlled in a large republic by a government that protects the public good.

47. **C**. Some states allow voters to petition to remove incumbents from office prematurely. In these cases, there would be a special election to determine if the official stays or is replaced.

48. **B**. A moderate-liberal or a moderate-conservative would be the best choice to balance this particular ticket. More likely, the moderate-liberal would be taken, but not always.

49. **B**. The Twenty-Second Amendment is the two-term limit for a President. Remember: Two 2's are in 22.

50. **E**. The President can't use extensive overseas force (for more than 60 days followed by a 30-day withdrawal period) without the consent of Congress. In addition, Congress must be consulted at least 48 hours before the military is deployed.

51. **E.** The power of the President has increased since 1941, as important foreign policy issues such as World War II and the Cold War have affected administrations.

52. **C.** In the ad hoc structure, task forces, committees, special advisors, and informal groups report directly to the President.

53. **B.** Ronald Reagan delivered on a campaign promise and appointed the first female justice, Sandra Day O'Connor, in 1981.

54. **A.** In *Marbury* v. *Madison*, John Marshall struck down a federal act for the first time ever. The process where the Supreme Court determines if a law is constitutional is called judicial review.

55. **D**. *Miranda* (due process rights) and *Gideon* (right to an attorney/counsel) both expanded rights of the accused.

56. **D**. Writs of certiorari are not granted commonly, as they are orders for lower courts to send up documents to the Supreme Court. The Supreme Court hears only a small percentage of cases.

57. **B**. Government corporations are run by the national government. Two examples are the Federal Deposit Insurance Corporation which insures bank deposits, and the Postal Service.

58. **B**. De facto segregation occurs when people voluntarily segregate themselves in residential areas. It is constitutional.

59. **A**. Uncontrollable spending (including entitlement programs such as Social Security) can't be eliminated from a budget.

60. **E**. The framers believed that the First Amendment built a "wall of separation" between Church and State. However, the Supreme Court has dealt with many cases concerning religion.

Now we're ready to begin!

NO BULL ~~NOBLE~~ REVIEW SHEET

Here are my Review Sheets. Use them often to help you study.

You will notice numbers in brackets after a word or sentence. These are the pages where you can find more detailed information.

Good luck!

Your friend,

Nobley

Most Important Terms of the Course (Numbers in brackets are reference pages in text)

1. Direct Democracy [5]
2. Republic [5]
3. Trustee [5]
4. Delegate [5]
5. Declaration of Independence [5-6]
6. Articles of Confederation [6]
7. Philadelphia Convention [6]
8. Great Compromise [6]
9. Commerce Clause [7]
10. Federalists and Anti-Federalists [7]
11. *Federalist Papers* [7]
12. *Federalist #10* [7]
13. Bill of Rights [7-8]
14. Federalism [9]
15. Elastic Clause [9-10]
16. Dual Federalism [10]
17. Cooperative Federalism [10]
18. Block Grants and Revenue Sharing [10]
19. Entitlement Programs [11]
20. Social Security [11]
21. Categorical Grants [10]
22. Mandate [11]
23. New Federalism [11]
24. Supremacy Clause [11]
25. Denied Powers [12]
26. Unwritten Constitution [13]
27. Formal and Informal Constitution [13]
28. Pluralist and Elitist Theories [13-14]
29. Political Socialization [19]
30. Cross-Pressured Voter [21]
31. Australian Ballot [21]
32. Public Opinion Polls [22]
33. Random Sample [22]
34. Activism [22-23]
35. Linkage Institution [28]
36. Political Party [28]
37. National Chairperson [30]
38. Political Machine [30-31]
39. Divided Government [31]
40. New Deal Coalition [29]
41. Minor/Third Party [30]
42. Interest Group [31]
43. Lobbying [31]
44. Revolving Door [31-32]
45. Grassroots Lobbying [32]
46. Litigation [33]
47. Public-Interest Group [33]
48. PAC [33-34]
49. Hard and Soft Campaign Money [34]
50. Super PAC [34]
51. Watchdog Media [36]
52. Press Secretary [35]
53. Horse-Race Journalism [36]
54. Speaker of the House [41]
55. Majority Leader [41]
56. Majority Whip [41]
57. Minority Leader [41]
58. Impeachment [42]
59. Incumbent [42]
60. Marginal and Safe Districts [42]
61. Franking Privilege [42]
62. Party Polarization [31]
63. Caucus (Congress) [47]
64. Caucus (Primary) [54]
65. Staff Agency [49]
66. Committee and Chairs [43]
67. Standing Committee [43]
68. Ways and Means Committee [43]
69. Rules Committee [43]
70. Appropriations Committee [43]
71. Bill [44]
72. Legislative Veto [46]
73. Filibuster [46]
74. Rider [46]

75. Logrolling [46]
76. Pork-Barrel Legislation [46]
77. Reapportionment [47]
78. Gerrymandering [47]
79. Initiative, Referendum, and Recall [49]
80. Line-Item Veto [44]
81. Pocket Veto [44-45]
82. Resolutions of Congress [46]
83. Open and Closed Primary [54]
84. Plurality and Winner-Take-All [55]
85. Nominating Convention [54-55]
86. Electoral College [55]
87. Balanced Ticket [56]
88. Executive Order [56]
89. War Powers Act [56]
90. Cabinet [57]
91. White House Staff [57]
92. EOP [57]
93. Independent Regulatory Agencies [57-59]
94. Federal Reserve Board [59, 76-77]
95. Legislative Oversight [59]
96. Advice and Consent [59]
97. Executive Privilege [59-60]
98. Presidential Approval Rating [60]
99. Presidential Succession [60]
100. Lame Duck [60-61]
101. Original/Appellate Jurisdiction [67]
102. Judicial Review [68]
103. Writ of Certiorari [68]
104. Original Intent and Living Constitution [68]
105. Judicial Activism and Judicial Restraint [69]
106. *Stare Decisis* [69]
107. Court Packing Scheme [69]
108. Plea Bargain [69]
109. Class Action Suit [69]
110. *Amicus Curiae* [70]
111. Public Policy [75]
112. Bureaucracy [75]
113. Merit System [75]
114. Bureaucratic Discretion [76]
115. Casework [76]
116. Monetary and Fiscal Policy [76-77]
117. National Debt [78]
118. Keynesian Economics [77-78]
119. Supply Side Economics [78]
120. Iron Triangle [79-80]
121. Issue Network [80]
122. Establishment Clause/Free Exercise Clause [86]
123. Wall of Separation [86]
124. Selective Incorporation [86-87]
125. Exclusionary Rule [87]
126. Jim Crow [88]
127. De Jure/De Facto Segregation [89]
128. Civil Disobedience [89]
129. Little Rock [89]
130. Affirmative Action [90]
131. Equal Rights Amendment [90]
132. Naturalization [91]

Know these terms and you will find success.

Key Questions

1. In what ways do people politically represent themselves? [5]
2. What purpose does each of the three branches have? [8]
3. What are specific main powers of each branch? [8]
4. What are the qualifications to hold major office? [8-9]
5. What types of federal grants should I know? [10-11]
6. What are the most important checks and balances to know? [12-13]
7. What ideologies do I need to know? What's a liberal? What's a conservative? [19]
8. Where do liberals and conservatives traditionally stand on issues? [20]
9. What shapes one's political attitude? [19-21]
10. How does the US compare to other nations in terms of voter turnout? [21]
11. What obstacles do voters face? [21-22]
12. What types of ballots should I know? [22]
13. What do I need to know about the history of political parties? [28-29]
14. How might candidates at the state level stray from the national party platform? [30]
15. What has happened to the number of interest groups over the last 60 years? [32]
16. What are some specific special interest groups to know, and what do they support? [32]
17. What forms of media are there? [34-35]
18. How does the media affect public policy? [36]
19. What is the relationship between the President and the media? [35]
20. What are the major powers of Congress? [41]
21. What are some major differences between the House and the Senate? [42]
22. What standing committees should I know? [43]
23. How does a bill become a law? [44-45]
24. How does the President win an Election? [54]
25. What are the major powers of the President? [56]
26. How is the Executive Branch configured? [58]
27. What is the structure of the federal court system? [66]
28. How does the Supreme Court operate? What other tidbits are relevant to know? [67, 68-69]
29. How might special interests affect Supreme Court appointments? [67]

30. Since the early twentieth century, what has happened to the size of the bureaucracy? [75-76]

31. What types of jobs make up the bureaucracy? [75]

32. How can the bureaucracy be checked? [76]

33. How is the federal budget created? [77]

34. What should I know about environmental, health care, and military policies? [78-79]

35. In what ways were African Americans denied the right to vote after ratification of the Fifteenth Amendment? [88-89]

36. How does one become a citizen? [91]

Federalism

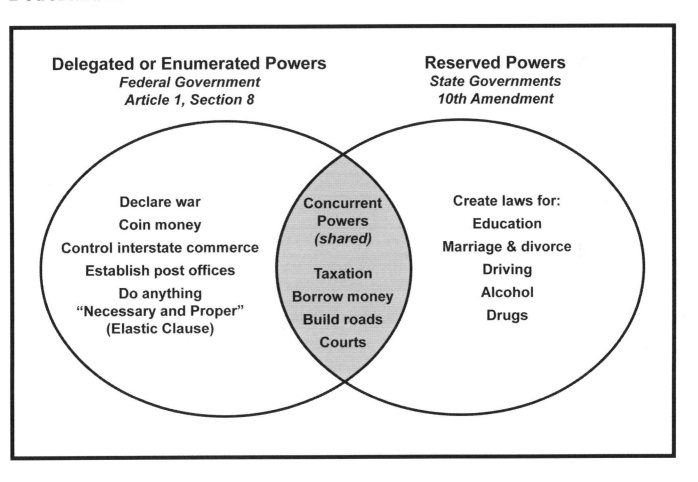

Checks and Balances

	LEGISLATIVE	EXECUTIVE	JUDICIAL
LEGISLATIVE CHECKS		1. Can override vetoes by 2/3 vote 2. Senate can refuse to confirm a Presidential appointment	1. Can change the size of the Supreme Court
EXECUTIVE CHECKS	1. Can veto bills 2. Can call Congress into special session		1. Appoints Supreme Court justices 2. Grants pardons and reprieves
JUDICIAL CHECKS	1. Can declare an act of Congress to be unconstitutional (judicial review)	1. Can declare an act of the President to be unconstitutional	

Amendments to Know

In Chapter 1 there's a review of how amendments are passed. Here are the most important ones.

Bill of Rights Amendments

1st Amendment - Freedoms of speech, press, religion, assembly, and right to petition the government.

2nd Amendment - Right to bear arms.

4th Amendment - Freedom from unreasonable searches and seizures.

5th Amendment - Due process rights (right to fair justice, and freedoms from self-incrimination). Also, one cannot be tried twice for the same crime. This is a freedom from "double-jeopardy."

6th Amendment - Right to a fair trial and attorney.

10th Amendment - Division of powers between the states and federal government (called federalism).

Civil War/Reconstruction Amendments
    13th Amendment - Abolition of Slavery.
    14th Amendment - Equality, Due Process Clause, and Equal Protection Under the Law.
    15th Amendment - Universal Male Suffrage.

Progressive Era Amendments
    16th Amendment - Graduated Income Tax.
    17th Amendment - Direct Election of Senators.
    19th Amendment - Women's Suffrage.

These Could Come Up As Well
    22nd Amendment - Two-Term Limit for Presidents.
    25th Amendment - Clarified succession of the President, and vacancy of Vice President's office.
    26th Amendment - Lowered the voting age to 18 in 1971, as Vietnam War soldiers were not old enough to vote.

Supreme Court Decisions

Cases Involving Federal and State Power
    Marbury v. *Madison*, 1803 - First use of judicial review. [67-68]

    McCulloch v. *Maryland*, 1819 - Maryland could not tax the Bank of the United States because of federal supremacy, and the right of the national government to charter a bank. [11-12]

    Gibbons v. *Ogden*, 1824 - The federal government is superior to the states and controls interstate commerce. [12]

Cases Involving Civil Rights
    Dred Scott v. *Sandford*, 1857 - Chief Justice Roger B. Taney said that slaves were property, and owners could not be deprived of them. [88]

    Plessy v. *Ferguson*, 1896 - Justified Jim Crow laws. *Separate but equal* was constitutional. [88]

    Brown v. *Board of Education of Topeka, Kansas*, 1954 - Ended segregation in schools. "Separate but equal" is inherently unequal. [89]

Cases Involving the First Amendment

Reynolds v. *US*, 1879 - Religion could not be used as a defense against polygamy, as the free exercise clause is not absolute. [86]

Schenck v. *US*, 1919 - Said that free speech was not absolute. One can't utter something that creates a "clear and present danger," as someone can't shout "FIRE!" in a crowded theater. [85]

Dennis v. *US*, 1951 - Upheld the Smith Act making it illegal to speak about overthrowing the government. Due process was limited because of a fear of communism. This was similar to "clear and present danger" of the *Schenck* case. [85]

NY Times Co. v. *Sullivan*, 1964 - Protected freedom of the press. Libel, or printing false statements against public officials, was only punishable if there was knowledge of the mistakes written, and intent to harm. Without such malice, damages could not be awarded.

Texas v. *Johnson*, 1989 - Burning of the American flag was protected by the First Amendment.

Oregon v. *Smith*, 1990 - Illegal drug use performed as part of a religious ceremony is still illegal drug use. [86]

Citizens United v. *Federal Election Commission*, 2010 - Overturned the part of the Bipartisan Campaign Reform Act which denied certain entities to run campaign ads before elections. [34]

Cases Involving the Fourteenth Amendment

Slaughterhouse Cases, 1873 - The Fourteenth Amendment did not protect slaughterhouse workers attempting to conduct a business. [88]

Korematsu v. *US*, 1944 - Japanese internment was constitutional, as in times of war, rights can be limited. [56]

Griswold v. *Connecticut*, 1965 - A Connecticut law making it illegal for married people to obtain contraceptives (birth control) was declared unconstitutional. The right of a married couple's privacy was protected. [91]

Miranda v. *Arizona*, 1966 *Gideon* v. *Wainwright* (1963), *Mapp* v. *Ohio* (1961) - All of these decisions of the Warren Court protected rights of the accused. [87]

Roe v. *Wade*, 1973 - Legalized abortion, but not in all cases. A woman's privacy was protected. [90-91]

Cases Involving Other Constitutional Issues

Baker v. *Carr*, 1962 - Federal courts can hear cases and force states to redraw district lines. [47]

Wesberry v. *Sanders*, and *Reynolds* v. *Sims*, 1964 - Further emphasized fairness as to how district lines are drawn. [47]

US v. *Nixon*, 1974 - President Richard Nixon was not protected by executive privilege, and had to hand over tape-recordings. Nixon remains the only President to resign the office. [59]

Buckley v. *Valeo*, 1976 - Campaign contributions are a form of free speech protected by the First Amendment. [34]

Gregg v. *Georgia*, 1976 - Chief Justice Warren Burger's Court decided that the death penalty does not automatically violate the Eighth (freedom from cruel and unusual punishment) and Fourteenth Amendments.

Regents of the University of California v. *Bakke*, 1978 - Race can be considered in the university admissions process, but distinct racial quotas are illegal. [90]

Bush v. *Gore*, 2000 - Ended hand-counting of ballots in Florida's Presidential Election. [68]

Cases Involving a School

Everson v. *Board of Education*, 1947 - Public busing to parochial schools was constitutional, as benefitting students was the main purpose of the law, and not the support of a religious institution. [86]

Engel v. *Vitale*, 1962 - The Supreme Court ruled that official school-sponsored prayer is a violation of the free exercise clause of the First Amendment. Even if the prayer was non-denominational and optional, it was still unconstitutional. [86]

Tinker v. *Des Moines*, 1969 - A student wanted to protest the Vietnam War, so he and some friends wore a black armband. They were suspended for making such a political statement. The Supreme Court ruled that clothing is an extension of free speech (First Amendment), and the students should not have been suspended.

Lemon v. *Kurtzman*, 1971 - The decision created the "Lemon Test" where a government's laws had to be secular, can't have the primary effect of advancing or inhibiting religion, and can't have entanglements with religion. [86]

New Jersey v. *T.L.O.*, 1985 - T.L.O. was a girl smoking in the school bathroom. The principal came in and confiscated her pocketbook which had rolling-papers for drugs and a list of contacts to sell them to. She was suspended. T.L.O. believed her rights were violated, and that the search was illegal. However, the Supreme Court ruled that in schools, search rights can be limited to protect the student body. This decision limited the Fourth Amendment rights of students.

Hazelwood v. *Kuhlmeier*, 1988 - This was another freedom of speech case. The school newspaper was printing material about the private lives of teenagers. Such information reported on included teen pregnancy and parental divorce. The principal deleted the controversial articles from the paper. Students felt their rights were violated and the case went as far as the Supreme Court. The court ruled that the principal was allowed to censor said materials to protect the rights and safety of minors.

Foreign Policy

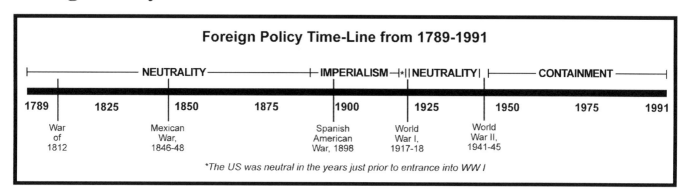

Important Acts and Policies

1. Judiciary Act of 1789 [68]

2. Pendleton Act [75]

3. Fair Labor Standards Act [87]

4. Executive Order 9066 [56]

5. Federal Regulation of Lobbying Act and Lobbying Disclosure Act [31]

6. Smith Act [85]

7. Civil Rights Act [89]

8. Voting Rights Act [90]

9. Gulf of Tonkin Resolution [79]

10. Freedom of Information Act [87]

11. Clean Air Act [78]

12. War Powers Act [56]

13. Federal Election Campaign Act [34]

14. Budget and Impoundment Control Act of 1974 [77]

15. Americans with Disabilities Act (ADA) [91]

16. Gramm-Rudman-Hollings Act/Balanced Budget and Emergency Deficit Control Act of 1985 [78]

17. Whistleblower Protection Act [87]

18. Brady Bill [87-88]

19. Don't Ask, Don't Tell [91]

20. Welfare Reform Act of 1996 [11]

21. Defense of Marriage Act [91]

22. Patriot Act [88]

23. Bipartisan Campaign Reform Act [34]

24. Affordable Care Act [79]

25. Budget Control Act of 2011 [78]

Notes:

Made in the USA
Lexington, KY
24 September 2013